Dot Com Profits

8 Steps to Building Unlimited Online Wealth

Ivan Ho

CONTENT

Foreword

As a person who has dedicated my life to helping people achieve their goals, I find this book to be an outstanding resource. In *Dot Com Profits*, Ivan Ho reveals the step-by-step strategies used by high achievers to generate massive online wealth. People typically have to pay a premium price for access to this type of information. That is why I could barely believe my eyes when I read this book. Ivan is practically giving away the world-class strategies of top Internet entrepreneurs.

From finding a buying market to generating high-quality traffic, ***Dot Com Profits* is the most comprehensive book on Internet wealth generation that I have ever read**. Using Ivan's 8-step system, you are equipped with all of the tools required to transform from a complete newbie into a money-making marketing machine in just a few pages.

I declare *Dot Com Profits* as the new bible of online wealth generation. It provides you with a proven blueprint so that you can avoid pitfalls and fast-track your online success. My favorite thing about this book is the real-life case studies. The numerous examples of people utilizing each strategy help you better understand how to apply these strategies to your business. The case studies give you an insider's glimpse into the minds of some of the world's most sophisticated online business owners.

Including valuable charts, graphs, and screenshots, this book over-delivers on its promises. Get ready to quadruple your income and create unlimited online wealth with *Dot Com Profits* by Ivan Ho. It just might be one of the smartest investments you ever make.

– Raymond Aaron, *New York Times* bestselling author

Introduction:

Generating Wealth

Within this book are the secrets to creating unlimited online wealth. The truth is that generating dot com profits is easy—as long as you have the right blueprint. If you have been following bad advice, then you may believe that making money on the Internet is hard to do, requiring years of blogging without pay and receiving little traffic to your websites(s). You may believe that you have to sacrifice time with your family and friends in order to learn how to make money online. But the truth is that you do not have to.

Generating online wealth is fun and easy. It allows you to make money in your sleep and live the life of your dreams. Building a profitable online business can give you the freedom to quit your soul-sucking job, relieve stress, and even buy a home with an ocean view! But you can only achieve these goals if you learn from the right people. The fastest way to create unlimited online wealth is to follow the blueprint of someone who has already done it. That person is me.

For the past decade, I have been making serious cash on the Internet by helping people just like you turn average ideas into extraordinary income. Stop living someone else's life and begin creating online wealth today.

Is this the right book for me?

Generating online wealth begins with a decision. You must decide that you are ready to take back your power and live life on your own terms. If you desire to create more freedom in your life, then this book is for you. In fact, this book is for anyone who is:

– Interested in making money online.

– Starting, or has recently started an online business.

– Searching for the blueprint to creating wealth.

– Interested in making a 6- or 7-figure income per year.

– Fed up with corporate nonsense.

– Interested in sharing your expertise online.

– Ready to break the link between your time and your money.

Regardless of your age, race, occupation or gender, this book will help you create massive online wealth. Whether you are fed up with your salary or interested in paying off your mortgage early, the principles in this book can help you reach your financial goals.

After reading this book, there is no turning back. Internet business owners are notorious for getting hooked on the 24/7 profit-generating machine known as the World Wide Web. Making money on the Internet is exhilarating! It will allow you to gain a freedom that you never thought was possible. Building a profitable online business will allow you to live the life that you have always wanted. Read on to discover what you will learn in this book.

Chapter 1: Find a Buying Market

In Chapter 1, I explain how to find a buying market. This means that I will help you validate your idea *before* you start your business (or before you make plans to expand your current business). This chapter will teach you how to find people who are ravenous for your products. Stop "guessing" what people want and start *knowing* for certain by using the strategies in this chapter. In addition to identifying a profitable niche, you will also learn:

- Why 80% of new businesses fail within the first 18 months (and how to *not* become one of them).

- How to get people to pay for your product *before* you create it.

- How knowing your customers' hopes and dreams can transform your business.

Chapter 2: Positioning & Branding

In Chapter 2, you will learn how to effectively position your brand at the top of your market. You will learn how to build authority, highlight your uniqueness, and exude credibility as you become the go-to expert in your industry. This chapter will show you how to own your niche and make your customers say, "Wow!" In addition to learning how to position your brand, you will also discover:

- The one action that will make people trust you instantly.

- How to differentiate yourself in a crowded market.

- How to establish an emotional connection with your audience.

Chapter 3: Selling High-Priced Offers

In Chapter 3, you will learn how to sell high-priced offers. I will help you understand why people are willing to pay high prices for certain products. This chapter will teach you how to use your newly-acquired skill of brand positioning to sell premium products with high profit margins. In addition to selling high-priced offers, you will also learn:

- How to turn free content into a premium offer.

- The top-secret psychological tactic that will bring a tenfold increase in your sales and wow your customers.

- How to turn your knowledge and skills into massive online wealth.

Chapter 4: Multiple Streams of Income

In Chapter 4, you will learn how to create multiple streams of income. You will learn how to make money off other people's products. You will also learn how to get other people to promote *your* products. In addition to creating multiple revenue streams, this chapter will help you discover:

- How to make money online 24 hours per day, 7 days per week.

- How to break the link between your time and your money.

- How to create a series of products that simultaneously promote one another and quadruple your earning potential!

Chapter 5: Automation & Streamlining

In Chapter 5, you will learn how to automate and systematize your business. This chapter shows you how to delegate time-consuming activities and create more freedom in your business. It shows you how to build a team of professionals to help you move your business forward. In addition to building a team, you will also discover:

- How to build marketing systems that make you money in your sleep.

- How to outsource your headaches and focus on profit maximization.

- How to leverage technology to scale your business (while you are on vacation in Hawaii!).

Chapter 6: Traffic Generation

In Chapter 6, you will learn how to generate traffic. This means that you will discover how to get your ideal customers to notice your products. This chapter shows you how to find qualified people to go through your sales process. In addition to generating traffic, this chapter will also teach you:

- Exactly where to find your ideal customers.

- How to avoid losing money on ads and instead actually get paid to run them.

- How to create a database of repeat customers who buy from you over and over again.

Chapter 7: Get Coaching

In Chapter Seven, you gain an understanding of why it is important to have a coach. You will learn how to find a mentor who matches your personality, so that you can follow his/her blueprint and achieve your goals much faster than you could alone. In addition to finding a coach, this chapter will help you:

- Understand how to properly approach a mentor (without risking rejection).

- Avoid amateur mistakes and better navigate the inevitable pitfalls that come with building an Internet-based business.

- Fast-track your online success by following a proven system.

Chapter 8: Bet on Yourself

In Chapter 8, you will learn why it is important to bet on yourself while you're on your entrepreneurial journey. This chapter will teach you how to dream big, work smart, and take back control of your life. In addition to betting on yourself, this chapter will also help you discover:

- The Number One trait that all successful people have in common.

- How to leverage other people's time and money in order to build the business of your dreams.

- How to expand your online business into a global enterprise.

In order to create unlimited online wealth, you must be willing to take action. This book can only help you if you apply its principles. If you take action by following the proven strategies, then you will be well on your path to dot com profits.

Now, let's get started on your journey!

Chapter 1:

Find a Buying Market

Finding a buying market is the first step to creating unlimited online wealth. According to Bloomberg, approximately 80% of new businesses fail within the first 18 months. One reason this occurs is because the entrepreneur failed to validate his idea. When you find a buying market and validate your concept *before* starting a business, you are almost guaranteed to succeed. In this chapter, I will teach you how to find people who are ravenous for your products. Eliminate the guesswork and find people who are happy to pay you money.

Validate Your Market

In order to avoid being one of the 8 out of 10 entrepreneurs who fail, you must first validate your market. This prevents you from hoping and guessing that your products will succeed. Instead, you will gain instant insight as to whether your idea has a buying market. Some of the best tools for validating your idea are the Amazon marketplace, pay-per-click advertising, Follow.net, keyword research, audience pre-sales, and targeted surveys.

Get Pre-sales

Getting pre-sales may be the best predictor of a product's success. Instead of spending months (or even years!) developing a product, the smart thing to do is to gain interest for your product before you even begin to create it. This is where a lot of Internet entrepreneurs get it wrong. I know countless people who have spent years writing "the next bestselling book" or developing a "revolutionary" online course, only to get minimal sales and disappointing results. Don't fall into this trap. Avoid trying to be a revolutionary, and focus on being an intelligent businessperson. A revolutionary *thinks* he has a great idea (and sometimes, he's right). An intelligent businessperson *knows* he has the right idea because he follows a proven system (and he's always right!).

The following case study showcases an intelligent businessperson who has validated his market by getting pre-sales for his product.

Case Study: John Lee Dumas

Entrepreneur on Fire founder John Lee Dumas never develops a product unless he has $10,000 in pre-sales. After failing numerous times in the past, he decided that this would be a good metric to go by. The following is an inside glimpse as to how John Lee Dumas validated his idea. While reading this, think about how you could apply these principles in your own business.

Prior to launching his product Podcasters' Paradise, John created a landing page where people could sign up if they were interested.

Podcasters' Paradise
Where you can go to learn how to:
Create ~ Grow ~ Monetize
Your Podcast

Why Podcasters' Paradise?

- ✓ **Video Tutorials**
  Whether you are a beginner, intermediate or expert podcaster, *Podcasters' Paradise* has the video tutorials you need to CREATE, GROW, and MONETIZE your podcast!

- ✓ **Forum**
  Looking to exchange honest feedback with other Podcasters? Chat about the latest tips, tools, and tactics? Share reviews in iTunes? Find other like-minded Entrepreneurs to interview and be interviewed by? The forum at *Podcasters' Paradise* has it all!

- ✓ **Monthly Webinars**
  Today's top podcasting experts will share their insights on what's working for them right now. These webinars will be ACTION-PACKED, recorded and placed within *Podcaster's Paradise* for you. Watch live or come back over and over again for the replay.

After creating the landing page, John shared his sales letter via his weekly newsletter and social media. As a result, over 240 people signed up to his list over the next five days. Yes! This means that people are interested. But John didn't stop there. He knew that *saying* you were interested was very different from *being* interested. Because of this, John emailed those 240 people with a $197 offer into his community. After only 72 hours, 35 members signed up. This resulted in almost $7,000 in sales!

After 4 more weeks of selling his product at a slightly higher price point, John found that 114 people had joined his community. This resulted in over $26,000 in sales. Wow! These are the results of idea validation. Instead of spending months developing a product and hoping that people would buy it, John validated his idea and got people to pay for it months in advance. Getting pre-sales for your product is an excellent way to validate your idea.

But what if I don't have an audience?

If you don't have an email list of 10,000 people to send traffic to your landing page, that's OK. In fact, Dane Maxwell and Andy Drish of The Foundation teach people how to build 6-figure software companies in 6 months or less entirely from scratch. Most of their students start out with no money, no experience, and no email list. Therefore, you have no excuses!

At The Foundation, Dane and Andy teach a concept called *idea extraction*. This occurs when a student in their program calls prospective clients and asks them questions about the biggest pains in their business. After collecting several different data points, the student then gets the prospective client to fund the software's development before they even create it! You don't have to be an established authority. You can validate your market and get your project funded with or without an email list. So, let's get started. Validate your market and create massive online wealth today!

Pay-per-click Advertisements

Another way to find a buying market is to observe pay-per-click ads. If people are spending money on advertisements, then there is a good chance that a significant amount of money can be made in that market. In fact, wine expert Gary Vaynerchuk has a popular online video in which he shows his video blog viewers how to find advertisers for their blogs. In the video, Gary simply types the word "beer" into Google and clicks on one of the advertisements. He then proceeds to call the contact number on the company's website.

After the owner picks up the phone, Gary asks if she would be interested in advertising on his new beer blog. The business owner agrees, and Gary instantly has a paid sponsor for his non-existent new Web show about beer. Amazing! This is the power of market validation.

Ads ⓘ

The Republic of Tea
www.republicoftea.com/
Shop Our Premium Tea Selection.
Enjoy Our $3.99 Flat Rate Shipping!

Shop For Tea Online
www.adagio.com/
Free shipping over $49!
Hundreds of farm-fresh teas.

Keyword Research

Another great way to find a buying market and generate wealth is to do keyword research. One of the most effective (and most affordable) ways to perform keyword research is to use the website Follow.net. After signing up with this website, you will gain access to a plethora of analytical tools that will help you validate your market. The keyword-related tools are among the most valuable.

Search Engine Optimization

Top Keywords

iSpionage

the top 5 keywords are hidden, unlock them here

	Keyword	Google Rank	Yahoo / Bing Rank
6	amazing life changing quotes	1	4
7	to make good money while	1	4
8	2 make money online	1	5
9	success quotes for women	1	5
10	make cash while sleeping	1	6

All you have to do is search for a particular domain in your field and identify its most commonly used keywords. Follow.net will even show you your biggest competitors. This will allow you to validate your idea and create products based on terms that your target market is already searching for. Follow.net is a powerful tool!

Top Yahoo / Bing SEO Competitors

the top 5 competitors are hidden, unlock them here

iSpionage

	Competitor	SEO Value
6	money.howstuffworks.com	$2,531,735
7	oprah.com	$1,322,641
8	money.ca.msn.com	$149,904
9	johnchow.com	$138,683
10	definitivewebsites.com	$27,388

Top Google US SEO Competitors

the top 5 competitors are hidden, unlock them here

semrush

	Competitor	Competition Level	Common Keywords	SE Keywords
6	yourlifeyourway.net		553	-
7	quotesnsmiles.com		659	-
8	motivationgrid.com		509	-
9	quotery.com		586	-
10	boardofwisdom.com		1,046	-

Amazon Marketplace

Using the Amazon.com marketplace is a fantastic way to validate your market. You can determine whether a market is worth your effort based on the number of products it has and the number of reviews for each product. For example, let's search for the keywords "make money online." Numerous products with hundreds of reviews show up! Therefore, the *make money online* niche is a proven market. Check out the search results below.

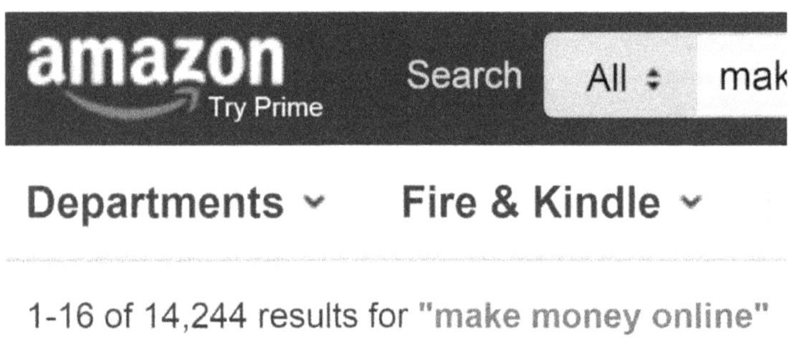

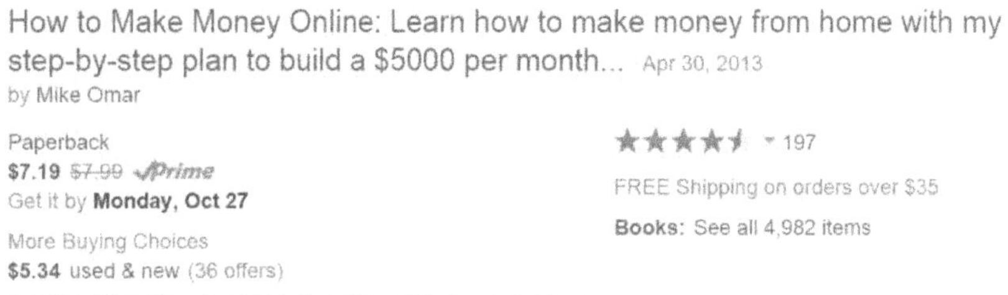

How to Make Money Online: Learn how to make money from home with my step-by-step plan to build a $5000 per month... Apr 30, 2013
by Mike Omar

Paperback
$7.19 ~~$7.99~~ Prime
Get it by **Monday, Oct 27**

More Buying Choices
$5.34 used & new (36 offers)

197

FREE Shipping on orders over $35

Books: See all 4,982 items

After you have validated your market, view the sales pages of the top products and scroll down to the negative reviews. After reading a handful of 1- and 2-star reviews, you will have a better understanding of what a particular market wants. The negative reviews showcase a product's shortcomings. They explain how a product failed to meet a customer's expectations. This is a marketer's dream! Just create a better product and your idea will already be validated! For example, the following review states that the book shown in the screenshot above is poorly written. The reviewer mentions that he/she desires a book with clear instructions:

2 of 3 people found the following review helpful

Poorly written, December 24, 2013

By **A Customer** - See all my reviews

Verified Purchase (What's this?)

This review is from: **How to Make Money Online: Learn how to make money from home with my step-by-step plan to build a $5000 per month passive income website portfolio (of ... each) (THE MAKE MONEY FROM HOME LIONS CLUB) (Paperback)**

This book is a disappointment. It is poorly written and doesn't have clear steps. It is just scrambled instructions for success using tools that don't work as described in the book. I don't recommend buying this.

If you were to write a book about making money online that had clear action steps, then your idea would already be validated and you could begin the process of creating serious online wealth. As long as the same criticism is repeated throughout several different reviews, you have completed the first step to finding a buying market.

All you would have to do next is create a better product. Once you have done this, the market is yours for the taking!

Understand Your Market

Understanding your market is essential to creating online wealth. Knowing your ideal customers' demographics and psychographics will help you avoid wasting time, money, and energy pursuing the wrong customers. Once you know exactly who you are targeting, building a profitable online business becomes much easier.

"If you want to sell what John Smith buys, then you've got to see through John Smith's eyes."

—Eben Pagan, Multi-millionaire Internet entrepreneur

Demographics

Identifying a clear demographic is essential to generating massive online wealth. If you don't know who you are targeting, then your marketing messages become obsolete! People with different demographics desire very different things. Internet millionaire Frank Kern says it like this: "A product that will teach a man how to attract the woman of his dreams will be more valuable to a 50-year-old man with no children who was divorced and desperately wants a family so he can continue his legacy and have all the things in life that a family represents to him than it would be to the average 21-year-old man who most likely only wants sex."

For this reason, it is essential that you know your target market's age, location, race, gender, and income. Depending on what you are selling, some factors are more important than others. However, age and gender are almost always the most important data points.

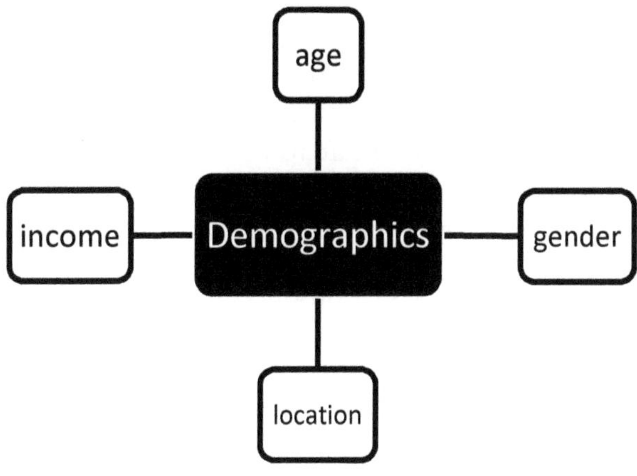

Psychographics

Demographics are important; however, psychographics are even more important. This crucial component is often overlooked by most online business owners. In order to *really* sell online products, you must understand the primary motivation of your target market. You must know what they value. A truly magnificent offer speaks to your prospect's pain points, their frustrations, their challenges, and their aspirations.

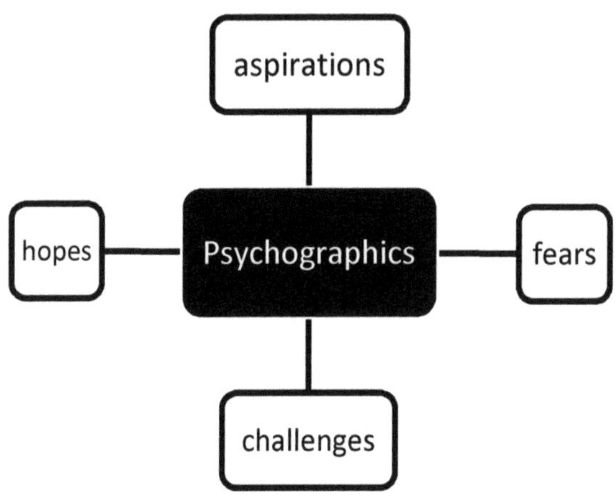

Once you know what *really* matters to your target market, you will be able to better name your products and services. In the words of Internet millionaire Brendon Burchard, "Marketing is 30% pain and 70% aspiration. Communicate to your customers' deepest desires." Therefore, you should always name your products based on who your prospects desire to *become.*

Some great examples of products named based on customer aspiration are as follows:

The Millionaire Messenger. This book targets experts who desire to make a fortune selling their advice. Authors, public speakers, doctors, accountants, consultants, and experts from every industry imaginable aspire to become a "millionaire messenger."

The Laptop Millionaire. Everyone wants to be a millionaire! If your product name includes the words "rich" or "millionaire," then you are far more likely to sell it. I dare you to find a person who does not desire financial independence.

6-Figure Consultants. Once again, the emphasis is on money. Everyone wants to make 6 figures per year (unless you are already making 7 or 8 figures).

America's Next Top Model. This show targets aspiring models who "want to be on top," as the opening credits explain. Every new model aspires to be the next "*it* girl," walking down runways in Paris wearing Calvin Klein swimwear. What a wonderful name for a show!

American Idol. Almost every singer alive aspires to be idolized by millions of fans worldwide. Not only do they want to be famous, but they want to be the "American Idol."

Top Chef. No one wants to be the "bottom chef." Competition is fierce in the restaurant industry, and winning on this show means that you are at the top!

Someone who knows exactly what her target market wants is Selena Soo of The Publicity Mastermind. After having extensive conversations with her clients, Selena realized the following:

> "Most of my clients want to be seen as the next great thought leader, to write a *New York Times* bestseller and to be interviewed on Oprah's *Super Soul Sunday*.
>
> When I am introducing myself to someone new, I say, 'I work with visionary experts, authors, and coaches in the 'live your best life' space, who are the next generation of Oprah personalities — the next Suze Orman, Brené Brown, Rachael Ray, or Dr. Oz.'
>
> My ideal clients get excited because not only am I **speaking to their deepest desires**, but I am also associating my work with powerful brands and personalities that have a high value in the marketplace."

Wow! Now that's someone who understands her market. I'll tell you more about the results of Selena's efforts in Chapter 3.

How do you get to know your customers?

There are several ways to better understand your market. One way is to simply listen to them. Read your emails. Pay close attention to blog comments and social media mentions. Listen for buzz words, and watch out for trends. Survey your prospects using tools such as SurveyMonkey. All of these strategies will help you better understand your target market and make serious money online. In addition to these tactics, a great way to understand your market is to simply *ask* them what they need help with.

The following is a great example of someone who asked their prospects what they wanted.

Case Study: Daniel DiPiazza

While brainstorming potential products to create, Daniel DiPiazza of Rich 20 Something decided to ask his audience what they wanted. In fact, he published a blog post titled, "What's Your Biggest Challenge?"

> ### So I'd like to know: What's your biggest challenge right now?
>
> - What's stopping your from launching a business, project or idea that you care about?
> - What have you tried in the past, and why didn't it work?
>
> **Please leave a comment below and let me know.**
>
> I'm looking for a TON of responses on this post, guys. I really want to dig in and get some feedback from the community — so please take 30 seconds and leave a comment below. It doesn't matter if you think your comment has already been answered, or if you think it's "stupid."
>
> I guarantee, it's not.
>
> Think you can help me out? It'd really mean a lot to me.
>
> Thanks!

After extensively polling his audience, Daniel realized that the people who made up his market primarily wanted to make more money. This realization led him to develop a high-end product that helped his audience make $1,000 per month on the side by freelancing online. This is the ultimate validation! I'll tell you more about the results of Daniel's efforts in Chapter 3.

Create Your Customer Avatar

Once you have validated your market and identified your ideal customer's demographics and psychographics, you are one step closer to building serious online wealth. At this point, the only thing you have left to do in this area is to create your customer avatar, which is simply a detailed description of your ideal client. After combining all of the information you've gathered so far, you should have a clear picture of your avatar. It even helps to give him/her a name. The following is a great example of a customer avatar:

Let's say that you're considering writing a book titled, *How to Quit Your Job and Travel the World.* You plan to target people 24-29 years old who are fed up with the rat race, tired of paying off student loans, and itching to feel free again.

In this case, your avatar's name is Alex. He is 25 years old with a degree in finance. He has been working on Wall Street for the past three years, and he hates it. Alex is frustrated because he spends 60 hours per week screaming on the floor of the New York Stock Exchange. He doesn't have time to enjoy his family and friends. He gave up his life for money, and he regrets it. His deepest desire is to be free. Alex dreams of telling all of his investment banking higher-ups to "shove it" as he boards a plane to Paris.

After discovering all this, you may consider changing the title of your book to *The Book of Freedom: A Step-by-Step Guide to Quitting Your Job and Traveling the World.* This way, Alex's primary desire for freedom will make him magnetic to your product.

This is how well you need to know your target market. This is how vivid their daily lives should be in your mind. Once you completely understand who you are targeting, you can then craft marketing messages that inspire them to act. But this can only be accomplished by applying the principles in this chapter.

Chapter 2:

Positioning & Branding

The right positioning and branding will fast-track your success in online business. If you want to create unlimited online wealth, then you need to position yourself and your brand at "top market." You have to build authority, highlight your uniqueness, and share your story.

Share Your Story

Sharing your story makes you and your brand more relatable. It establishes an emotional connection with your audience, which makes them more inclined to trust you. Instead of seeing you as an untouchable guru, your market will see you as an old friend. When sharing your story, you should focus on defining moments. Be sure to highlight your challenges, your obstacles, your wins, your losses, your failures, and your "Aha!" moments. The more authentic your story, the more of a connection you will have with your audience. Few people share their story better than Oprah Winfrey:

Case Study: Oprah Winfrey

Oprah Winfrey is a media proprietor with a classic rags-to-riches story. She often tells the story of being a poor little African-American girl raised on a farm in Mississippi. Her grandmother, who was a maid, said that her dream for Oprah was to simply find a good family to work for. This means that Oprah's grandmother thought she would follow in her footsteps and become a maid!

The media icon frequently discusses how she was molested at a young age. Oprah even openly discusses her challenges with weight. Over the years, we have seen her go from size small to size medium to size large over and over again! Millions of people can relate to this struggle. We all have experienced weight fluctuations, regardless of whether or not they were this extreme.

Oprah has gone from being a poor little girl in Mississippi to a billion-dollar businesswoman. In 2008, she even campaigned with the man who is now President of the United States! Oprah's story is both inspiring and relatable. Regardless of how rich she becomes, her audience will always see her as one of them—a woman who has excelled in the face of adversity. Now, that's a good story!

Develop Your USP

In order to position your brand at top market, you must have a unique selling proposition, or USP. A unique selling proposition is simply something that makes you different or better than your competitors. It distinguishes you from the pack. A great USP can be a phrase or a tagline that accurately describes your brand. It explains the results you get for your customers, and establishes you as an authority. The following are wonderful examples of effective USPs:

The Millionaire Maker. Wealth coach Loral Langemeier claims to have created hundreds of millionaires; therefore the moniker "the millionaire maker" perfectly describes her brand and sets her apart from other wealth coaches.

The Gen Y Guy. As a result of branding himself "The Gen Y Guy," Jason Dorsey became the go-to expert on millennials. If your organization targets this particular age group, then how could you not hire The Gen Y Guy? He owns the niche!

The Millionaire Matchmaker. Third generation relationship expert Patti Stanger has a national television show on the Bravo network named after her USP. If you are a wealthy man or woman looking for love, then you would look to none other than "the millionaire matchmaker" for help. It's a no-brainer!

Live Your Best Life. Oprah Winfrey makes her mission clear with the tagline of *O, The Oprah Magazine*. It is evident from the front cover that her brand exists to help people live better lives.

Think Different. Personified in its renowned 1984 Super Bowl commercial, Apple Computer is a company that thinks different. This slogan implies that they are not like all of those other computer companies.

The Happiest Place on Earth. As the tagline for Disneyland, this USP is genius! Every kid wants to go to "the happiest place on Earth" to have fun. And if a kid wants it, a parent gets it!

Become an Expert

One of the best ways to generate online wealth is to position yourself as an expert in your field. A person with expertise is automatically more credible and trustworthy than the average guy on the street. The perception of expertise is why we trust doctors, lawyers, and accountants. Without credentials and experience, no one would trust their advice! This psychological principle also applies online. You don't have to have a Ph.D., but you do need to know your subject matter.

Write a Book

The fastest way to build a brand and become an authority is to write a book. Few distinctions are more credible than that of an author. When you literally "write the book" on a subject, you are instantly regarded as an authority. If you don't consider yourself to be a writer, that's OK. In Chapter 5, I will tell you how to find qualified people to help you write your book. In the meantime, however, here is a case study explaining how writing a book can transform your business:

Case Study: Matthew Hussey

For years, Matthew Hussey struggled to make it as a dating coach. He worked out of coffee shops in London and made YouTube videos to get noticed. At one point, he was even sleeping in his office because he couldn't afford rent for both an apartment and an office space! Matthew created numerous products and programs, but nothing seemed to be giving him the international exposure that he so desperately craved.

After several years in business, Matthew finally landed a book deal. After his book *Get the Guy* hit No. 10 on *The New York Times* bestseller list, he became a regular contributor to *The Today Show*, got cast as a relationship expert on NBC's *Ready for Love*, and even got his own show on iHeartRadio! Currently, Matthew hosts high-end seminars and retreats all around the world. None of this happened until he wrote a book.

Does that mean I need to write a bestseller?

Just for clarification, you do not have to write an international bestseller in order to become an authority. Heck, you could self-publish your book and sell zero copies! Either way, you will still be regarded as more of an expert than someone who only has a blog. In the world of expertise, authority is everything.

Be Everywhere

Possibly the best way to position yourself as an authority is to be everywhere. Aim to get on every media platform you possibly can. Re-purpose your content, and associate yourself with high-quality brands. Few online entrepreneurs do this as well as Pat Flynn.

Case Study: Pat Flynn

Pat Flynn is the founder of Smart Passive Income, a website dedicated to helping people make an honest living online. He has a blog, a YouTube channel, and two podcasts. When he creates content, it gets uploaded to all 4 of his different platforms. After he publishes content, it then gets shared on every major social media platform in existence. This gives him higher perceived expertise, which makes him more trustworthy and more valuable to the marketplace.

Being everywhere has enabled Pat to gain a loyal following. In fact, his following is so loyal that they buy anything he recommends. In September 2014, Pat made $98,640 selling other people's products! His trustworthiness has enabled him to make a great living from niche websites and affiliate commissions. Both Pat's income and his fame exploded after he decided to be everywhere.

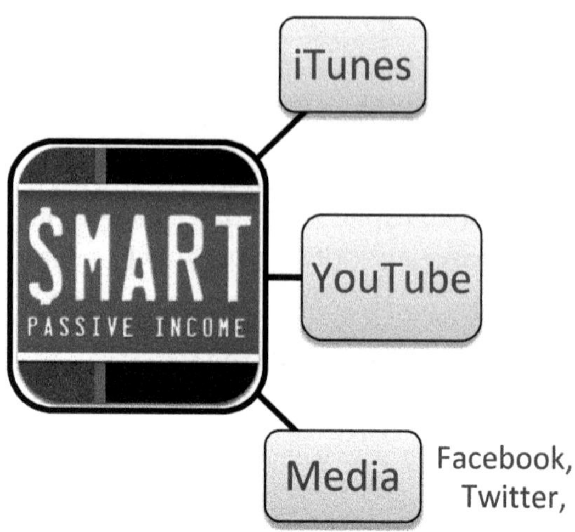

Brand Your Name

A great way to position yourself as an authority is to brand your name. When taking this approach, your name should be highlighted on everything you create. From books to courses to physical products, your name *is* your brand. Few people have branded their names better than Suze Orman.

Case Study: Suze Orman

Suze Orman has branded herself "America's most trusted financial advisor." She has spent over 30 years helping people manage their money and, as a result, she has built a personal branding empire. Her name is on books, television shows, magazine covers, bank cards, and even financial management software! Take a look at how Suze Orman has branded her name:

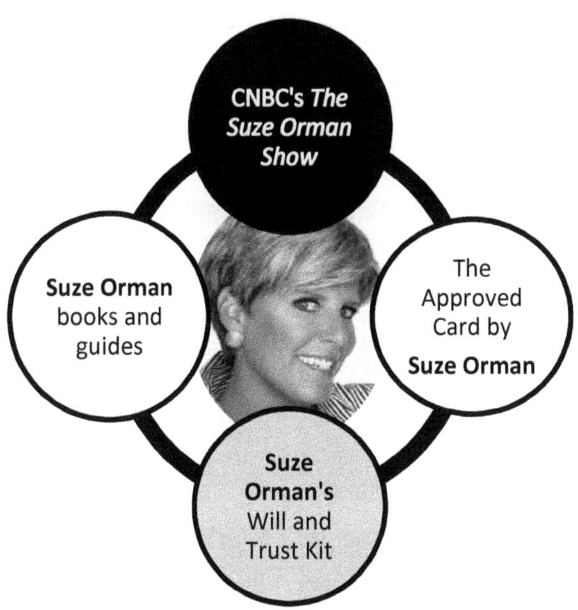

Brand Your Business

You can either brand your name or your business, but not both. Attempting to brand both entities simply confuses people. Richard Branson is a great example of someone who has branded his business. Take a look inside his Virgin empire:

Case Study: Virgin Group

Richard Branson's brand Virgin Group consists of over 400 different companies in a multitude of industries. Founded in 1970, Virgin Group owns businesses in areas ranging from travel to healthcare to telecommunications. In fact, the company was named "Virgin" because Branson would randomly start businesses in industries in which he had no experience! The following graph showcases an outstanding model for branding your business:

Deliver the Wow Factor

A great way to differentiate yourself is to make your customers say, "Wow!" You must add massive value and over-deliver on your promises. Nice gestures such as mailing thank-you letters or sending a box of cookies to your customers leaves a wonderful impression. The whole idea is to give them something they were not expecting. This will ensure that they never forget you.

"You get a car! You get a car! You get a car! Everybody gets a car!" These were the words spoken by Oprah Winfrey to celebrate the premiere of the 19th season of her talk show. After much anticipation, Oprah gave away new cars to all 276 people in her audience. The next day, every major media outlet was talking about it. Even though this occurred over a decade ago, it remains one of the most memorable moments in television history.

You don't have to give away cars, but you do need a "wow factor." Give your customers something they are not expecting. Give them fuel for word-of-mouth marketing.

Chapter 3:

Selling High-Priced Offers

The fastest way to create online wealth is to sell high-priced offers. High-priced products and services attract high-quality people. The price of your offer greatly depends on its modality. Text, audio, video, and in-person events all have different levels of value. (We'll talk more about this in Chapter 5.)

Audio- and video-based products have higher perceived value than text-based products such as books and newsletters. In-person events and one-on-one consulting have higher perceived value than any other modality.

People are willing to pay a high price for your time, your knowledge, your experience, and your network; therefore, you should consider offering premium products, consulting services, or a mastermind group as a part of your business model. Selena Soo makes a great living by providing premium consulting services:

Case Study: Selena Soo

Selena Soo is the founder of the Publicity Mastermind. After spending nearly 10 years developing her skills and building her network, Selena decided to strike out on her own. Because she has so many connections in the media industry, Selena decided to position herself as a premium service provider.

You may remember Selena from the section of Chapter 1 about understanding your target market. If you recall, Selena's clients want to be seen as "the next great thought leader." Because of this, Selena has pictures of herself with several other "great thought leaders" on her website. Now, that's great positioning!

As a result of her expertise (and her exceptional positioning), the revenue from Selena's consulting practice far exceeded her corporate salary within her first year in business! Selena has a few high-quality clients who each pay her $24,000 per year. Selling high-priced offers quickly made her a 6-figure consultant!

Create a High-Level Mastermind Group

A fantastic way to generate unlimited online wealth is to create a high-level mastermind group. Not only are people willing to pay for your knowledge, but they are also willing to pay for your network. Take a look at how Joe Polish monetizes his high-level mastermind group:

Case Study: Joe Polish

Joe Polish is the founder of the Genius Network Mastermind. This program is also known as the 25K Group because its members pay $25,000 per year to join! Members of the Genius Network Mastermind have quarterly meet-ups and group mentoring sessions that completely transform their businesses. In fact, Joe discourages anyone from renewing their membership if they did not make at least $100,000 as a result of the ideas presented during one of their quarterly gatherings.

Access to this group appears to be worth every penny, as members get to befriend multi-millionaire entrepreneurs such as Brendon Burchard, Dan Sullivan, Jeff Walker, Steve Forbes, and Arianna Huffington (founder of *The Huffington Post*). Members of the Genius Network Mastermind even get to hang out on Necker Island with Richard Branson! These opportunities are easily worth more than $25,000 per year.

Focus on High Profit Margins

In order to create unlimited online wealth, you must focus on high profit margins. It takes the same effort to get 10 high-quality customers as it does to get 10,000 lower quality customers. For example, authors who have a new book to launch typically do a lot of different kinds of promotion. They write for blogs, schedule interviews, launch advertising campaigns, organize speaking tours, and even hire publicists to get them on national television. However, if the author simply promoted a $1,000 training product instead of a

$10 book, he would have much better results. Take a look at the following graph to get a better understanding of this concept:

<table>
<tr><td>$10 book</td><td>x</td><td>10,000 customers</td><td>=</td><td rowspan="3">$100,000
in sales</td></tr>
<tr><td>$1,000 training product</td><td>x</td><td>100 customers</td><td>=</td></tr>
<tr><td>$10,000 course</td><td>x</td><td>10 customers</td><td>=</td></tr>
</table>

Many online business owners believe in promoting lower-cost products because they are easier to sell. Although this may be true, lower-priced products also mean lower profit margins. The effort required to sell a lower-priced product is actually the same as the effort required to sell a higher-priced product.

It is just as easy to sell something at $10 as it is to sell something at $1,000. Regardless of the price point, the sales process is the same. You will need a blog, a traffic generation system, a sales funnel, a shopping cart, a payment processor, and a delivery method regardless of the type of product you're selling.

Let's say you want to make $100,000 per year. You can either A) sell a $10 eBook, or B) sell a $1,000 tutorial program. Which one would you choose? Which one do you think would be the easiest path to 6 figures? Option A would require you to sell 10,000 eBooks. Option B would require you to sell 100 tutorial programs. With the $10 eBook, you would need to sell 100 times more products to equal the income generated by just one $1,000 tutorial program! This means that Option B would be the quickest path to online wealth.

It may take a little more effort to sell a $1,000 product than it does to sell a $10 product. It is possible that it will take 4, 5, or even

10 times more effort; however, it will never take 100 times more effort. Selling a $1,000 product will give you 100 times more income than a $10 eBook.

The selling process is the same, regardless of how much you charge for a product; however, the revenues you make are drastically different. Trying to make money with banner ads just doesn't cut it anymore. The profit margins are too low to sustain a viable income. So don't be afraid to promote expensive items or to create your own high-value products. As long as you have a quality product and a well-built marketing funnel, people will purchase your offer.

Who the heck is going to buy a $10,000 course?

You would be surprised by how much money people are willing to spend on a training course. Truthfully, it's not about the price; it's about the investment. Selling high-priced offers is all about perceived value. Education has ten times more perceived value than cars, clothes, and other luxury items because people see it as an investment in their future. If you don't believe that people will pay $10,000 for a course, then let's take a look at the higher education system.

18-year-old students fresh out of high school (who generally have absolutely *no money*) spend 4-8 years and $50,000-$250,000 on a college "education."

Most of them have no idea what they want to do with their lives, yet they still graduate with $30,000 of student loan debt that quickly turns into $100,000 after a few years of accumulated interest. This is like having a mortgage before you even get your first real job!

If they do happen to get a job, then it's probably not going to be that 6-figure job they were promised by their parents and teachers. A large percentage of college graduates end up working at minimum wage jobs like McDonald's, hating their lives and regretting their "investment."

Even with all of this evidence, students still go to college because of the promise that it will pay off. The *perception* of college being an "investment" pushes students to act irrationally and possibly suffer for the rest of their lives. This is the power of perceived value. Please use this power for good.

Case Study: Ramit Sethi

Ramit Sethi, author of *I Will Teach You to Be Rich*, sold his course, Earn 1K, for $1,000. His unique selling proposition (what you learned about in Chapter 2) was, "Earn 1K on the side using skills you already have or get your money back." Wow. That's quite a guarantee!

This was Ramit's rationale for selling such a high-end course: If a student earns an extra $1,000 per month from this course over the next five years, then that is worth a lot more than $1,000.

$1,000 x 12 months x 5 years = $60,000 of extra income

Even after just one year, students are poised to earn at least $12,000 on the side. This justifies the high price point and positions his product at top market. Suddenly, spending $1,000 in order to earn $60,000 seems like a pretty good deal!

This is the psychology of perception. Always highlight your customer's return on investment.

How do you go from free content to a premium offer?

Almost everything that you give away for free can be transformed into a premium offer. Whether in the form of a blog post, a book, or even an email series, turning a low-value product or service into a high-value offer only takes a small mindset shift and a little value stacking. Let's take a look at how Daniel DiPiazza turned his free content into a premium offer:

Case Study: Daniel DiPiazza

Daniel DiPiazza is the founder of Rich 20 Something. You may remember him from the section in Chapter 1 about understanding your target market. After working various low-paying jobs during his early 20s, Daniel decided that it was time for a change. In an effort to make some extra cash, he began searching for jobs on the popular freelancing website Elance. Luckily for Daniel, his efforts paid off. His company reportedly earned $23,700 on the freelancing platform in just 4 weeks! This prompted Daniel to quit his soul-sucking job as a waiter and go into online business full time.

Excited by his results, Daniel decided to share his experience in a popular article titled "Hacking Elance." This free article immediately went viral. It got tons of traffic, comments, and positive feedback. The article even got re-published on major blogs like The Huffington Post, Lifehack, and Under 30 CEO. This was the ultimate market validation!

With this newfound insight, Daniel turned that free article into a $497 course with over 60 students. He added over 15 hours of video content and provided in-depth information on each area of freelancing. After 15 months of development, Daniel turned his free article into $30,000 and counting!

Almost anything can be transformed into a premium offer. Simply go more in-depth and add more content. Spending some extra time on product development can create massive results.

Will people *really* buy my premium product?

Yes, people will *really* buy your high-end product as long as you effectively communicate its value. You must explain the serious amount of time and money that you have spent gathering this information. When people understand what you went through in order to attain the knowledge that you are about to teach them in your course, they immediately perceive it as a high-value offer.

Case Study: Marie Forleo

Online business titan Marie Forleo sells a $2,000 course that helps people build online businesses. She often emphasizes the fact that she has spent the last 15 years running her own business. Marie also mentions that she has spent thousands of dollars on books, courses, seminars, and mastermind sessions in order to learn everything that she is about to teach you in her 8-week video course. In other words, Marie's pitch is, "Spend 15 years and $100,000 to learn this information OR learn everything I know about online business in 8 weeks or less." Wow. That's quite a value proposition!

Marie also explains that her course is much more than just a bunch of videos. It contains templates, swipe files, worksheets, access to a members-only forum, and even the chance to get personalized help from Marie herself! In addition to all of this, students are also granted lifetime access to her program, which means that they receive free updates each year the program is active.

Marie's sales page is also full of video testimonials from people who have already improved their businesses as a result of the course. She also communicates her credibility by adding the logos of trusted brands that have featured her in the media:

B-SCHOOL

As seen in:

Forbes Entrepreneur WSJ

The New York Times

Mashable

Marie's 15 years of experience
+
A community of achievers

+

8 weeks of training videos

+

A long list of bonuses

+

Lifetime access

=

$10,000 of value for only $1,999

When you effectively communicate your product's value, people are more inclined to purchase your offer. Explain to your prospects the amount of time and money that you have spent in order to learn what you are about to teach them. Using these strategies will rapidly move you toward creating massive online wealth.

Chapter 4:

Multiple Streams of Income

In order to create unlimited online wealth, you need to have multiple streams of income. In today's world, you cannot rely on just one source of income. Products get outdated. Competition arises in the marketplace. Website traffic slows down, which results in a decrease in customer flow. In order to create a sense of financial security for your family, you need to have money coming in from a variety of different sources throughout the year.

Be sure to expand your product line vertically, going from online tutorial programs to coaching sessions to high-end retreats. Choose one area of expertise and expand upon that topic by creating multiple related products— until you have built an empire that makes you money in your sleep. (I'll go into more detail about how to do this in the next chapter.)

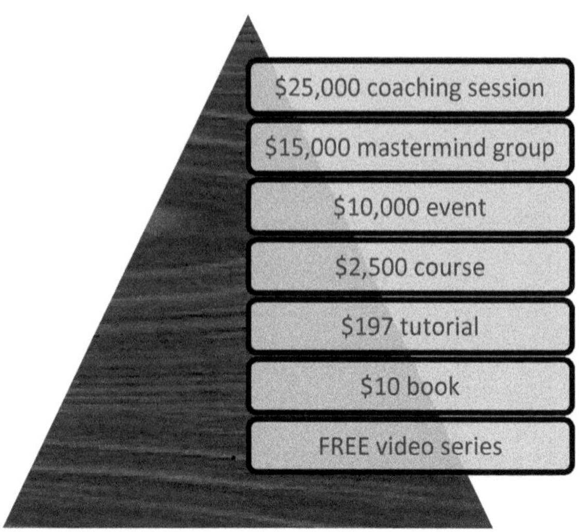

The whole purpose of creating multiple streams of income is to break the link between your time and your money. There are only 24 hours in a day; therefore, it is very difficult to make 7 figures per year based solely on the number of hours you work.

When you sell products online, there is no ceiling on your income. You are free to make as much money as you like. With multiple streams of online income, you can make money, whether you're reading to your children or on vacation in Paris. You can even make money in your sleep!

Because time is such a limited resource, you need to ensure that your wealth is unlimited. The way to create unlimited online wealth is to increase the amount of money you earn every hour by creating multiple streams of income. Diversifying your revenue model means that you are well on your way to creating dot com profits!

Multiple streams of income allow you to gain freedom and take back control of your life. They give you time to enjoy your family and to do the things that really make you happy. Time is a scarce resource. Once it's gone, you can never get it back. You can control money; however, the time we each have is often controlled by a power greater than ourselves. This is why you must create multiple streams of income.

You can create multiple streams of income regardless of the type of business you have. Even if you own an offline business with physical products, you can still create additional streams of revenue online. Take a look at how Trish Stratus has monetized her offline business:

Case Study: Trish Stratus

Trish Stratus is the founder of Stratusphere Yoga Studio. After sustaining a very serious back injury during her career as a professional wrestler, Trish turned to yoga for relief. After gaining first-hand experience of the healing effects of yoga, Trish decided that she wanted to spread the word about this life-changing practice. This led to the opening of Stratusphere Yoga Studio.

After 3 years of running her brick-and-mortar studio, Trish decided to expand into online business. She created her own brand of yoga DVDs, yoga mats, fitness gloves, and even a custom dumbbell set! Take a look at her product line, below:

PRODUCTS OVERVIEW

travelmat

dumbbellset

dvd

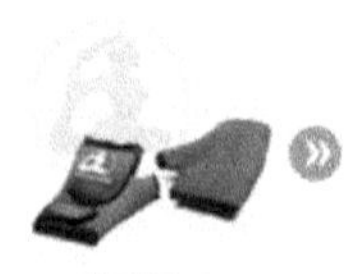
fitgloves

But her income streams don't stop there. Trish also sells T-shirts, magazines, posters, trading cards, phone cases, tea infusers, and tickets to meet-and-greets on her website. This is the holy grail of multiple revenue streams. The best thing about it is that her entire business model is based on a single theme: helping people become healthy and fit.

Affiliate Commissions

One of the easiest ways to create multiple streams of online income is to become an affiliate marketer. Large companies like Amazon.com have affiliate programs that you can easily join and start making money from immediately.

Email service providers like AWeber and web-hosting companies like Bluehost also offer attractive affiliate programs. When you become an affiliate for a company, you make money from each referred sale of their products. This means that you get paid every time someone clicks on your affiliate link and buys a product. You will either be paid a percentage of the sale or a standard dollar amount. For example, you can make $65 per referral with web-hosting company Bluehost. Let's take a look at how easy it is to sign up for their affiliate program:

<u>Step 1: Visit the company's website</u>. In this example, I am using Bluehost; however, the affiliate process is very similar for other websites such as Amazon, AWeber, Clickbank, and E-junkie.

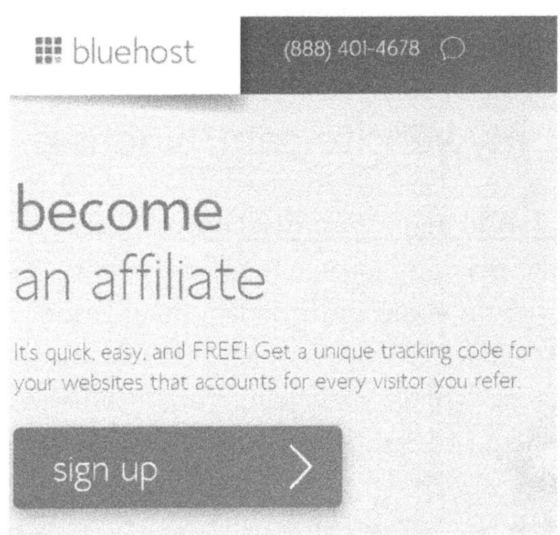

<u>Step 2: Begin the application process</u>. Fill in your username, your password, and your email address. Some programs even allow you to input your banking and tax information as a part of the initial application process. Depending on your preferred vendor, you may even be required to explain how you intend to promote the company's or the individual's products.

Affiliate Signup

Thanks for signing up to be an affiliate of Bluehost! You'll be paid for every visitor that signs up from your personalized tracking code

affiliate login information

Account Username

This name will appear in your referring link

Password

Confirm Password

account information

Step 3: Add your custom affiliate link to your website. If your application is approved, then you will be given a custom tracking link that confirms that a lead was referred by you. You may also be given access to advertisements that you can easily add to your website.

mywebsite.com/bluehost

Step 4: Add an affiliate disclaimer. Note: This is required by the Federal Trade Commission to inform visitors of your relationship with the company. Including an affiliate disclaimer increases trust and keeps you out of legal trouble. Remind your customers that you are recommending a product because it is beneficial to them, not because you receive a portion of the sales.

Disclosure: Please note that some of the links below are affiliate links, ***and at no additional cost to you****, I will earn a commission if you decide to make a purchase. Please understand that I have experience with all of these companies, and I recommend them because they are helpful and useful, not because of the small commissions I make if you decide to buy something. Please do not spend any money on these products unless you feel you need them or that they will help you achieve your goals.*

Step 5: Promote their products and make money! Affiliate promotions can be either passive or active. A passive affiliate promotion typically consists of including a product on your "Resources" page or in the sidebar of your website. Active promotions generally consist of writing blog posts or hosting webinars to sell products.

MY MOST RECOMMENDED

If you look at nothing else on this page, these are the four that you should know about. I find myself recommending these resources again and again, in emails and on podcasts. I use them because they make my life easier, and I'm confident you'll agree too.

Bluehost: 99% of my websites are hosted on Bluehost. Why? Because it's incredibly easy to use with 1-click automatic WordPress installation and *excellent* customer service – via phone and via chat. **I HIGHLY RECOMMEND** using Bluehost for your first site. Also, you can use the same hosting account for multiple domains if you plan on creating more websites. ***Click this link to get a special discount off the regular price!***

A great example of someone making money with affiliates is John Lee Dumas. Not only does he make a great living selling affiliate products, but he embodies the concept of creating multiple streams of online income. Let's take a look inside his business:

Case Study: John Lee Dumas

John Lee Dumas is the founder and host of Entrepreneur on Fire, a daily podcast where he interviews inspiring entrepreneurs. After only 2 years in business, his company generates over $200,000 per month.

John's public income report for September 2014 reveals that he has approximately 25 different income streams that include books, sponsorships, mentorships, mastermind groups, affiliate commissions, and high-end products. Here is the breakdown of Entrepreneur on Fire's revenue:

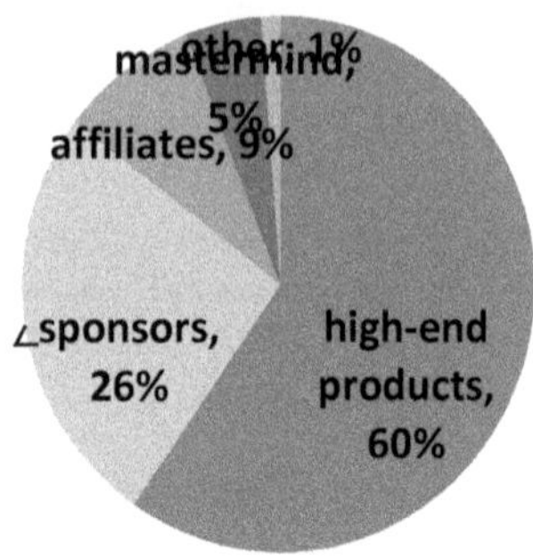

According to the report, $144,068 of Entrepreneur on Fire's revenue came from high-end product sales. (This proves the concept of selling high-priced offers from Chapter 3.) Another $62,167 of the company's revenue was from sponsors of John's Internet radio show (He practices the "be everywhere" principle that you learned about in Chapter 2.) According to the report, $20,918 of the company's revenue was from affiliate commissions. An elite mastermind accounted for $11,417 of revenue. John had only one consulting client that month, so mentoring accounted for $1,000 of his income. Book sales accounted for only $423 of revenue.

John has built these income streams by creating a vertical product line around the subject of podcasting. His book is titled *Podcast Launch*. He offers a podcast launch package. He runs Podcasters' Paradise, a community of podcasters. John even offers an elite mastermind just for high-level podcasters. This is how you vertically expand your product line. Choose one subject area and build multiple related products around that topic.

Get Other People to Promote Your Products

In addition to promoting other people's products, you can also get other people to promote *your* products. This mindset shift makes *you* the breadwinner in the affiliate relationship. When you have 100 other people promoting your products, this gives you an additional 100 streams of income. Your main focus should be on creating high-end offers and getting other people to promote them for you.

Curious about B-School? Here's my 100% honest review

Have you heard of Marie Forleo's B-School?

It is the best online business training program I know of.

Enrollment is now closed. Registration will likely open again in February or March 2015.

If you're interested in joining B-School through me next year, go here and enter your information.

In this review, I'm going to share with you what B-School is, why I love it, and who I think it's best suited for (and not for). I'm also going to tell you about exclusive bonus offers you can get if you sign up for B-School using my affiliate link.

If you're curious about B-School, keep reading. This is my 100% honest review of Marie's program.

Are you ready to join B-School?

If you're ready to take a leap in your business and make money online, I believe that Marie Forleo's B-School is the best business program out there.

Or maybe you have some questions? I'm here to help. Email me and I'll answer you honestly, even if that means recommending you don't enroll in B-School!

For example, Marie Forleo's online business program sells for $1,999. Each of her affiliates gets a 50% cut of the sales. This means that each affiliate earns $1,000 per sale. That is one heck of an incentive! The best thing about it is that Marie is actually the one profiting. The affiliate is making 50% of the profits, but Marie is making $1,000 passively!

This is the way to massive online wealth. Build multiple streams of income and get other people to promote your products. Unfortunately, none of this will work unless you have adequate systems in place. Learn how to systematize your business and make money in your sleep by reading the next chapter.

***Find out** how to use Multiple Streams of Income to increase your online profits. Just go to my website: www.DotComProfitBook.com and sign into the Bonus Area for a Free video tutorial.

Chapter 5:

Automation & Streamlining

In order to create unlimited online wealth, you must automate and systematize your business. The way to Internet riches is to generate income 24 hours per day, 7 days per week. You can only do this if you stop working *in* your business and start working *on* your business. This means that you must delegate time-consuming activities like email and customer service, so that you can focus on bigger tasks like creating additional revenue streams.

While streamlining your business, you must refrain from Superhero Syndrome—the disease of trying to do everything yourself. If you want to create unlimited online wealth, then you must build a team to help you reach your goals. **Your main job as an online business owner is to create systems that other people manage while you focus on creating additional revenue streams.** When you see yourself as a leader of a team rather than as a solo entrepreneur, you begin to break down mental roadblocks and move much faster toward dot com profits.

Build Your Team

In order to create unlimited online wealth, you must build a solid team. You need people to handle your email, your customer service complaints, your website design, and any other recurring or one-time activities that other people are better at doing than you are. You can hire virtual assistants, web designers, and other online professionals on popular websites like Elance, Fiverr, and Virtual Staff Finder.

Fiverr has branded itself "the marketplace for creative and professional services." On this platform, you can find qualified contractors to complete your projects on time even if you're on a budget. You can find someone to design your logo, edit your video, or even write your sales page for only $5! Fiverr is like a convenience store. It's the ideal place to go if you are working on a small project; however, you should consider using Elance for bigger projects, simply because the price of a project usually reflects the quality of work.

Founded by outsourcing expert Chris Ducker (the man who coined the term "Superhero Syndrome"), Virtual Staff Finder will connect you with full-time virtual assistants in the Philippines. Using this service will ensure that you find an excellent assistant to manage the daily operations of your company while you focus on developing additional revenue streams. This company is very different from both Fiverr and Elance. Virtual Staff

Finder is not a place for one-time projects. It is a place to find a long-term team member. You cannot simply get a logo or a website designed on this platform. Use Virtual Staff Finder only if you are looking to employ a full-time virtual assistant in the Philippines to help you with the daily operations of your company.

Elance®

Elance is the most popular online staffing website in the world. With a database of over two million freelancers, you are sure to find a good team member on this platform. Elance is my Number One recommendation for outsourcing large projects. If you need video narration, copywriting, or even website design, then Elance is the place to find high-quality professionals. Just create an account, post a job, and watch as dozens of qualified contractors compete for the opportunity to work with you. Let's take a look at how easy it can be to hire your first assistant:

Step 1: Log on to Elance.com. In this example, I am using Elance.com; however, each platform has a similar process. After you have chosen your preferred platform, you can begin creating an account.

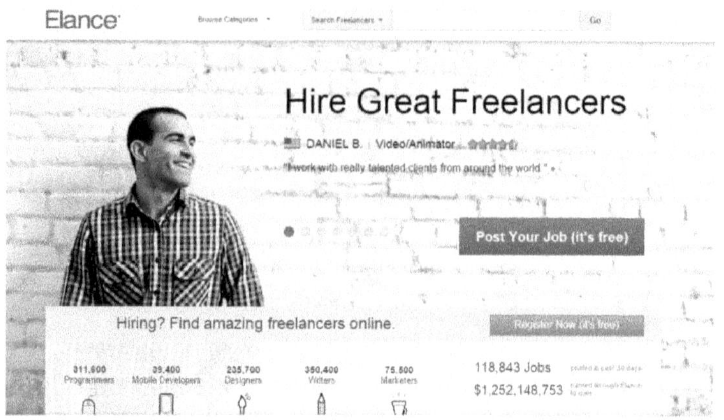

Step 2: Create an account. Enter your name, your email address, your physical address, your proposed username and password, and any additional information that is needed to get started.

Create an Account

Looking for work? **Sign up as a Freelancer.** Have an account? **Sign In.**

Use my info from: facebook Linkedin

First Name Last Name

Email Address (See our strict Privacy Policy.)

Username

Password Retype Password

Continue

By clicking, you agree to our Elance Terms of Service

Step 3: Post your job requirements. Be very specific about the type of person you are looking to hire. Include character traits, background requirements, and a description of what the job entails.

Advanced Virtual Assistant

Admin Support > Virtual Assistant

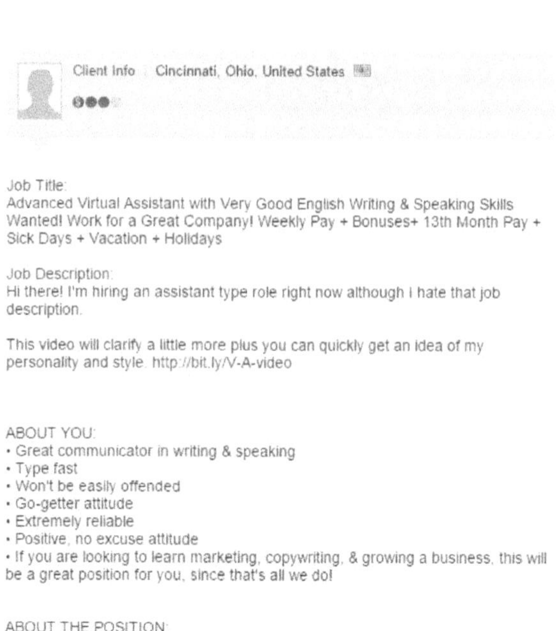

Client Info Cincinnati, Ohio, United States

Job Title:
Advanced Virtual Assistant with Very Good English Writing & Speaking Skills Wanted! Work for a Great Company! Weekly Pay + Bonuses+ 13th Month Pay + Sick Days + Vacation + Holidays

Job Description:
Hi there! I'm hiring an assistant type role right now although I hate that job description.

This video will clarify a little more plus you can quickly get an idea of my personality and style. http://bit.ly/V-A-video

ABOUT YOU:
- Great communicator in writing & speaking
- Type fast
- Won't be easily offended
- Go-getter attitude
- Extremely reliable
- Positive, no excuse attitude
- If you are looking to learn marketing, copywriting, & growing a business, this will be a great position for you, since that's all we do!

ABOUT THE POSITION:
- Write articles for me & posting them on our sites
- Handle Social Media Postings both for our company and customers
- Handle customer service emails
- Handle daily operations tasks
- Create sales emails & send them to prospects
- Do online research
- Work 4 hours a day 5 days a week

Step 4: Choose the best proposal. Immediately after posting your job, dozens of freelancers will begin to submit their proposals. Consider a contractor's experience, their proven skill set, and their public portfolio when deciding to pursue a partnership. You should also schedule a Skype or phone call before hiring someone for a big project. This will allow you to get a better feel for their personality, ensuring that you have chosen the right person for the job.

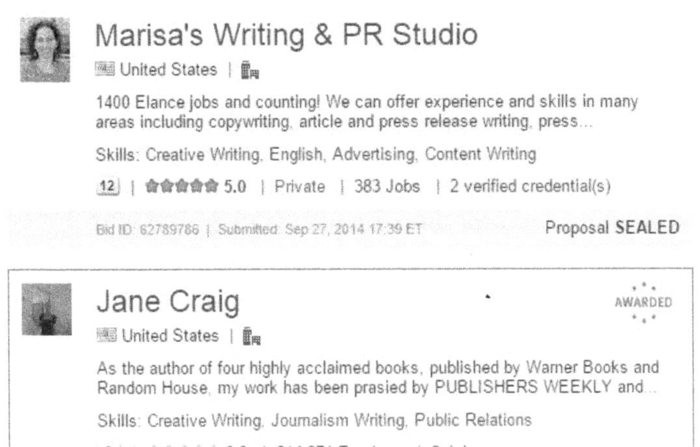

Step 5: Assign work to your new team member. After you have chosen the right person for the job, simply complete any necessary paperwork and introduce them to the rest of your team. Hiring a team member on any of these platforms is a fairly simple process.

You should consider outsourcing anything that you cannot do proficiently yourself. If completing a series of tasks would not be the best possible use of your time, then hire an expert to do it for you. Avoid Superhero Syndrome and hire people more capable of completing your crucial business projects. This will allow you to get your online business profitable much sooner.

Building a solid team will get you to dot com profits a lot faster than trying to do everything yourself. Using the tools I've just outlined, you can hire qualified people from almost anywhere in the world to help you build your business. Hiring these professionals will allow you to manage your project from start to finish, rather than stressing out over small details that you shouldn't be working on in the first place!

In Chapter 2, I explained how writing a book is critical to your positioning and branding. By using one of the outsourcing platforms we've just reviewed, you can find someone to help you write a book (even if you don't consider yourself a writer). This is how Nicklas Kingo outsourced his book-writing projects while building his online empire:

Case Study: Nicklas Kingo

Nicklas Kingo is a fashion model who makes passive income online by selling books. According to his April 2014 interview on The Side Hustle Show, Nicklas makes an average of $1,500 per month online without having to do very much work. Now, I know you're reading this book to learn how to create massive online wealth, so $1,500 per month may not seem like a lot of money; however, the fact that Nicklas generates this income *passively* while **outsourcing all of the work** makes this case study worth reading. Making $1,500 per month from books you don't even write sounds like a pretty good deal to me! Let's take a look at how Nicklas created this passive income stream:

According to the interview, Nicklas hires writers on Elance to write books for $35-$120. He then hires a contractor on Fiverr to design the book cover for $5. This means that the average cost of producing one of his books is less than $100. Nick then sells the 50-page book for $2.99 on Amazon.com. While receiving a 70% royalty, he only has to sell 50 copies to make back his initial investment. At the time of this interview, Nick had released 15 different books. This means that he makes an average of $100 from each book every single month.

The holy grail of online income is to get someone else to write the books that act as a lead magnet for your higher-priced offers. I'll tell you more about how to use books to sell higher-priced products in the next case study. In the meantime, however, learn how to systematize your business to create massive online wealth.

Systematize Your Business

After you have begun building your team, it is essential to systematize your business. Eliminate the guesswork and get your team to create "street-level" documents. These documents illustrate the step-by-step procedure for every critical function in your business. They are called "street-level" documents because anyone from off the street should be able to easily understand and implement the outlined procedures. A great example of a "street-level" document would be my explanation of how to join a company's affiliate program in Chapter 4, where I gave you a simple outline with screenshots to show you how to start making money by selling other people's products.

Another great example would be my example, above, of how to hire a contractor on Elance. Make sure that your street-level documents are actionable and easy-to-understand. Online personal growth publishing company Mindvalley keeps a database of their business procedures in Google Docs. Doing this makes it easy to train a new employee if a member of your current team gets hit by a bus. Before requesting the development of these documents, assure the members of your team that no one is being replaced. Be sure to explain that systematizing the business makes it easier on all of you.

Build Sales Funnels

One of the best ways to create unlimited online wealth is to build marketing sales funnels. These funnels automate and streamline every viable income stream in your business. In order to create these funnels, you can use customer relationship management (CRM) software such as Infusionsoft and Office Autopilot. These tools allow you to automate and scale your business. They give you the ultimate leverage by allowing you to upsell additional products by creating email follow-up campaigns that make you more money. One world-class expert at creating sales funnels is Brendon Burchard:

Case Study: Brendon Burchard

Brendon Burchard is a multi-millionaire Internet entrepreneur. Brendon is famous for coining the term "integrated product suite," which is simply a collection of related products, each of which solves a different problem or satisfies a different need for your target market. For example, Brendon wrote a book called *The Millionaire Messenger*.

He has also created several products that help experts monetize their knowledge. He has produced audio programs on productivity, advanced speaker training, and even high performance courses. These are all tools and resources that his audience of experts can use to grow their business. Let's take a look at how Brendon leads customers through his sales funnel.

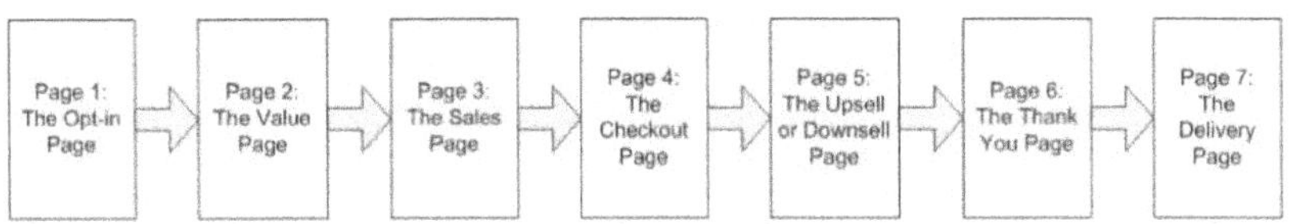

Brendon typically begins his sales funnel by leading prospects to a landing page that contains a free video. This video always adds massive value and creates immediate results for the prospects.

The prospect then proceeds to enter his or her contact information so that they can be sent a free book. They only have to pay for shipping and handling. This allows Brendon to capture the customer's name, email address, and physical address so that he can upsell additional products throughout the lifespan of this newly-formed relationship.

Immediately after the customer purchases the book, Brendon upsells him or her on a related product. A customer is more likely to purchase a product immediately after having just purchased another product. Brendon reportedly had an 18% conversion rate on this $197 upsell. These conversions funded the book giveaway.

After the initial upsell, the customer is then put through the remainder of Brendon's sales funnel. After about a week (and 3 more highly valuable videos), he offers a higher-priced training course. After a few more weeks, the customer is sent a direct mail invitation to one of his events. If the lead purchases a ticket, then he or she is offered a membership into a high-level mastermind group. After several months in Brendon's sales funnel, a customer is even offered a personal coaching session.

Following Brendon's blueprint by creating an integrated product suite is a fantastic way to generate online wealth. After you create the suite, set up automated systems to scale your business. Applying these principles will set you well on your path to dot com profits; however, none of this will work unless you have qualified traffic going to your offers. Learn how to generate traffic in the next chapter.

***Learn** how to setup a high converting Sales Funnel using Leadpages in just 30 minutes. Just go to my website: www.DotComProfitBook.com and sign into the Bonus area for a **Free video tutorial**.

Chapter 6:

Traffic Generation

In order to create unlimited online wealth, you must have qualified leads going through your sales funnel at all times. The only way to ensure that this occurs is to generate traffic. Traffic is the life-line of your online business. Your product will not make you any money unless you have qualified leads going to your offer. In other words, the income you earn is in direct proportion to the amount of traffic you generate.

The fastest way to generate targeted traffic is to buy ads. Purchasing advertising space from search engines like Google, Yahoo!, and Bing, or social media sites like Facebook, Twitter, and LinkedIn is the easiest way to increase your sales and kickstart your online business income.

You may be afraid to spend money on ads for a lot of different reasons. I've found in my experience that most people are afraid to advertise because they are either scared of losing money or because they've had bad results in the past. After reading this chapter, you will understand how to use paid traffic without fear. Continue reading to learn how to leverage paid traffic to build your online business.

Focus on Paid Traffic

In order to create unlimited online wealth, you must focus on paid traffic. You can buy customers using search engine pay-per-click (PPC) ads. You can even buy customers using social media. Paying for traffic allows you to test and validate your market immediately. Instead of guessing or assuming what a market segment wants, paid traffic allows you to verify your hypothesis in a short amount of time.

Generating organic traffic from search engines, blog posts, and social media is very time-consuming. It takes hours to create content and years to build an audience on social media. Free traffic sources are also very inconsistent. Your traffic may spike after you publish a new blog post, but then it levels off during the rest of the week. Paid traffic, however, creates instant results! When you begin a paid campaign, you know immediately whether or not it's paying off. This is why you should not be afraid to spend money.

As noted above, people typically avoid paid traffic either because they are afraid to lose money or because they've experienced bad results when they used it in the past. You, on the other hand, will never have to worry about losing money if you use the methods that I'm about to teach you. Don't let recent results wear you down or stress you out. There are plenty of ways to use paid traffic to advance your business. If you apply the strategies in this section, you will no longer have to worry about losing money.

If you have lost money in the past by using ads (or if you just didn't feel like it worked), then you may have been doing it incorrectly. It is possible that you were under the guidance of someone who didn't quite understand the value of testing. If you test your ad campaign with a small amount of capital, then you will never have to worry about losing money in the long term. This is why it is important to calculate your return on investment (ROI).

Know Your ROI

When dealing with paid traffic, it is essential that you know your return on investment. If you have lost money in the past, then it was most likely because you were not accurately checking your ROI. Testing paid traffic immediately tells you whether or not you have a winning campaign. If you simply throw a pile of cash at ads, then how can you expect to profit from them? Put only a small amount of cash into ads in the beginning. Track your profits and losses to determine whether or not to continue with the advertising campaign.

For example, you should consider spending $100 to test an ad. If the ad converts, then invest $1,000 in it. If the ad still converts, then scale it. If the ad does not give you a return on investment, then consider adjusting the offer, the copy, the target audience, or even the advertising channel. Using paid advertisements does not have to be risky. Simply test and adjust accordingly.

It's OKto spend $1 in order to make $3. That's a 200% return on investment! In this case, you would be earning $2 for every

$1 you spend! There are very few investments that can give you that kind of a return. It's also OK to spend $100 to get $150 (although you might want to consider testing for higher profit margins). Spend money as long as you are making money. Any ad that gives you a return on investment should be kept for the rest of eternity. Continue to optimize for maximum ROI; however, you should always keep an ad until you begin to lose money. **Spending money in order to make even more money is the key to unlimited online wealth.**

The Two Most Important Paid Traffic Sources

The two most important paid traffic sources are search engines and social media. In order to expedite your journey to dot com profits, you must be willing to maximize these two channels. Search engine pay-per-click ads can give you an attractive ROI. Social media ads have also been proven to quickly create wealth. Utilizing both of these traffic sources can rapidly move you toward your goal of unlimited online income. Let's take a closer look at these search engine and social media advertising platforms.

Search Engines

The three major search engines are Google, Yahoo!, and Bing. You can use these platforms to set up pay-per-click advertisements to scale your business. Although I will not go into detail about the technical aspects of search engine ads, I will use this section of the book to give you an overview of the different benefits and drawbacks of each platform. The following is a brief summary of the Google, Yahoo!, and Bing advertising platforms:

With 70% of the market share, Google is the most popular platform on the Web for pay-per-click advertisements. The company's flagship program, Google AdWords, allows you to attract more customers and grow your online sales. The user interface allows you to advertise to a global audience. With Google AdWords, you only pay when someone clicks on your ad. The cost of advertising is solely dependent upon your budget. Because Google is in such high demand, this platform is also the most expensive.

Yahoo! is the second most popular search engine on the Web. Although the company dominates as an email service provider, its ad program is lesser known. The way Yahoo!'s Ad Manager program works is very similar to other search engine advertising platforms. You simply sign up for an account, set your own budget, track your performance, and reach new customers. Because Yahoo! ranks second in the search engine market, your advertising costs will generally be lower than on Google. This means that you can experience the same results with Yahoo! as you can with Google—but for a much lower price!

Still relatively new to the marketplace, Bing has taken the search engine market by storm. Developed by

Microsoft, Bing Ads allow you to geo-target your top customers. This means that you can target your audience based on their location. Bing also highlights its universal event tracking system, which allows you to track customer conversions. Having the least popular search engine (of the three mentioned here in this section) means that advertising costs are relatively low compared to Google. Often, you can even get similar results for a lower price.

Social Media

One of the best ways to generate online wealth is to advertise on social media. Some of the most popular social media platforms include Facebook, Twitter, and LinkedIn. Each platform serves a specific purpose that, in turn, determines how well your advertising methods work. In order to succeed with social media advertising, you must understand the dynamics of each platform. For example, LinkedIn is more of a professional network, while Facebook is more of a traditional social network where people go to make friends. Twitter is more focused on its trending topics rather than its users. The following is an overview of each social network and its advertising capabilities:

Facebook is a social platform with over one billion users worldwide. This platform focuses on the personal lives of its users through its use of friend requests, likes, sharing, and timelines. People frequently use Facebook to reunite with old friends. Using Facebook ads, you can target customers based on location, behaviors, interests, connections, and demographics. This means that you can optimize your marketing efforts by advertising directly to your customer avatar. Facebook's world-class targeting system allows you to find customers based on their age, their gender, their hobbies, and even their personal network. The only pitfall to using Facebook ads is that they exist on a very social platform. This means that users are typically more interested in connecting with their friends than being offered a product.

Twitter is a social media platform based on trending topics. Users on this platform generally spend most of their time on the site looking through their news feed for updates and for information on current events. Twitter advertising generally does not work very well, simply because your business has to compete with millions of other data points just to get your prospects' attention. Despite its drawbacks, a Twitter ad allows you to easily analyze customer behavior and optimize your campaign performance in real time.

With over 310 million members worldwide, LinkedIn is the premier social network for business professionals. LinkedIn ads target small business owners, decision-makers, and corporate executives all around the world. The ability to target your audience based on job title, industry, seniority, and company size is what really sets LinkedIn apart from its competition. The fact that LinkedIn has a database of millions of business professionals with higher-than-average incomes makes it the ideal place to advertise high-value offers.

Collect Contact Information

In order to create unlimited online wealth, you need to have repeat buyers. This means that you need to capture the email addresses of each of your customers. In the long term, capturing contact information will save you money and get you to dot com profits much sooner. In addition to gaining new leads with your advertising efforts, you will also have a "house list" of customers who already know, like, and trust you. Having an email list makes it much easier to sell future products.

Regardless of what you may believe, email marketing still works. Email allows you to build relationships with each customer by offering him or her valuable information over and over again. It removes all gatekeepers and allows you to communicate directly to your target audience. Collecting email addresses gives you a database of repeat customers. Repeat customers are the ticket to online wealth.

The following case study is a great example of someone who built a database of repeat customers. Not only has this person done a wonderful job at collecting email addresses, but she has applied almost every other principle discussed in this chapter. Let's take a look at how Valerie Shoopman used paid traffic to generate massive revenue:

Case Study: Valerie Shoopman

This case study exemplifies almost every principle mentioned in this chapter. It perfectly illustrates how to run a successful advertising campaign with a high ROI. Pay close attention to how Valerie collected contact information, tracked her return on investment, and avoided losing money in pursuit of new clients.

According to an interview conducted on the ConversionCast podcast, Facebook marketing expert Valerie Shoopman teamed up with business coach Nick Unsworth to generate $61,000 in just 4 days — using Facebook ads. They reportedly spent only $5,269.40 to drive all of their advertising traffic to two high-value webinars. In other words, they spent just over $5,000 to generate $61,000 in sales. That's an 1129% return on investment!

Valerie reportedly sold 25 seats to a $997 live training event, and Nick gained a $3,000 per month elite coaching client. The combination of these sales is what generated all of this income.

$997	x	25 seats	=	$25,000
$3,000	x	12 months	=	+36,000
				$61,000

According to the interview, Nick and Valerie's $997 offer consisted of 20 days of Facebook ad training. During the first 10 days, Nick offered training on business strategies such as lead magnets, sales funnels, and positioning. During the last 10 days, Valerie offered her expertise on the technical aspects of Facebook marketing, such as image placement and conversion tracking.

The Facebook ad appeared in the news feed of prospects who were targeted during the initial setup process. It contains a picture of both Valerie and Nick with a simple description of their offer. Because Facebook only allows for text to take up 20% of an ad's photo, most of the text is displayed within the description.

When someone clicked on their ad, the prospect was then taken to a landing page in order to collect his contact information so that he could be reminded of the live training. This put the prospect into their sales funnel and allowed Nick and Valerie to add value long before the webinar even began. Valerie decided to use the same picture of both Nick and her to create a sense of brand consistency. This strategy emphasizes safety and increases trust. At this point, the prospect is already registered for the event. The only thing left for him to do is to actually attend the webinar.

What You'll Learn...

- Step-by-step process how to run and optimize Facebook ads so that you can get high quality likes, leads, and new customers. Literally everything you need to be successful, A to Z!
- How to get targeted "Likes" for just a penny each and how to get targeted email opt-ins for less than $2 each.
- How to navigate Facebook's new changes to their advertising platform and a simple process for how to track and manage your campaigns.
- "Target Your Email" list strategy - increase conversions by running targeted ads to your email list via Facebook.

In order to track return on investment, Valerie set up a conversion tracking pixel within Facebook's user interface for both the opt-in page and the sales page. A conversion tracking pixel is simply a tracking code that reveals your traffic sources. It allows you to track your cost per lead and eliminate low-converting ads.

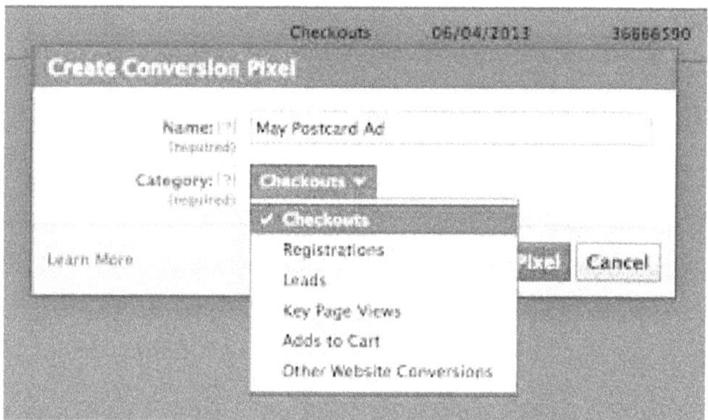

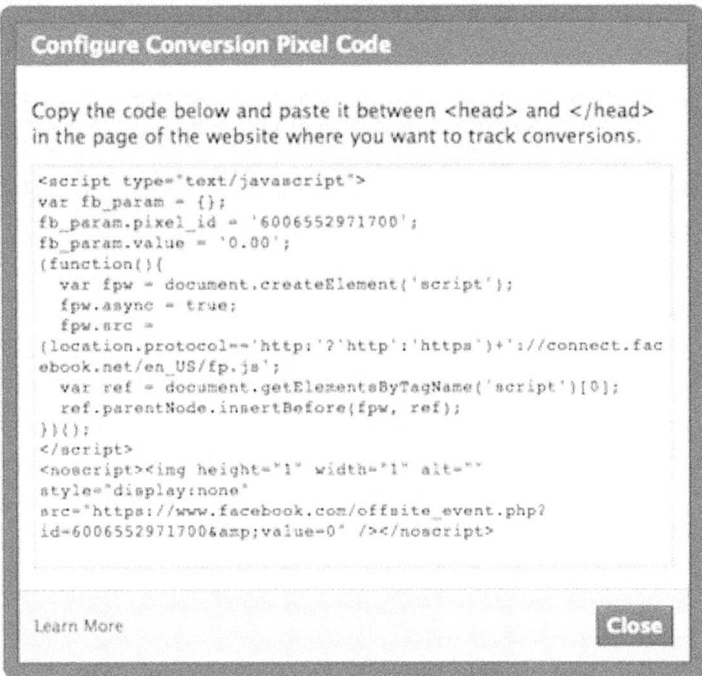

Using these strategies allowed Valerie and Nick to turn $5,000 into $61,000 in just 4 days! They got a 1,129% return on investment simply by applying the principles mentioned in this chapter. The only thing you have to do next is to get coaching. Read on to the next chapter to discover how finding a mentor can skyrocket your online wealth.

***Learn** my secret strategy on how to use Facebook Ads to get a ton of traffic. Just go to my website: www.DotComProfitBook.com and sign into the Bonus area for a **Free video tutorial**.

Chapter 7:

Get Coaching

Not only should you be offering coaching as an additional income stream, but you should also be *receiving* coaching. This is essential for creating serious online wealth. Learning from someone who has already accomplished what you desire to achieve will fast-track your success. You need a coach or a mentor so that you can follow their blueprint. This will allow you to emulate their success and achieve your goals much faster than you would otherwise.

Be sure to seek coaching from a mentor, not an advisor. It is often said that an advisor has the ingredients, but not the recipe. In other words, an advisor has all of the information required to succeed, but he or she does not know how to put it all together. Ingredients are useless without a recipe! Advisors often lack personal experience in an industry; therefore, you should avoid the coaching of an advisor.

A mentor, however, generally has years of experience doing what you want to do. A true mentor has experienced the inevitable pitfalls that come with building a business. Mentors have learned from their failures, and they are adept at helping you avoid making the same mistakes.

According to a study of over 100 self-made millionaires, 54% of them had a mentor to help guide them. The other 46% wished they'd had a mentor because they would've gotten there sooner! Get coaching immediately if you want to create unlimited online wealth.

Case Study: John Lee Dumas

I know I've mentioned John Lee Dumas more than once in this book; that's because there's a lot to learn from this online rock star! From getting pre-sales to validate your market to creating multiple streams of income, John is a wonderful example of online business done right. But it wasn't always this way.

Before John Lee Dumas was a podcaster extraordinaire, he was an army officer-turned real estate agent who was fed up with the daily grind. When he decided that he wanted to start his own Internet radio show, he sought the counsel of podcast veteran Jamie Tardy. However, her coaching was not cheap. John paid Jamie $1,000 per month for one-on-one coaching. Within the first three months of his mentorship, Jamie took John to the most important industry events and introduced him to key influencers. Shortly after these introductions, he had already booked the first round of guests for his new show!

The next several months consisted of John building his audience and creating additional revenue streams. As a result, John became a millionaire after only two years in business! Wow. These are the results of getting a mentor.

Sign up for coaching from someone you admire. Make sure that they are where you want to be. Get them to show you the blueprint, and you could be the next Internet millionaire!

Why You Should Have a Mentor

Having a coach or a mentor helps keep you accountable. Aside from providing a blueprint for you to follow, mentors also help you avoid procrastination. If you try to create online wealth by yourself, it may take you years of trial and error. Mentors and coaches save you time and help make your business profitable much sooner than it would be otherwise.

How to Find a Mentor

When searching for a coach or a mentor, it is essential that he or she be the right fit for you. You should look for mentors who have already accomplished what you desire to achieve. Your coach should fit your personality.

In order to find the right coach for you, simply take an inventory of your favorite books, courses, or events. If you genuinely enjoyed reading someone's book, taking someone's course, or hearing someone speak at a conference, then there is a good chance that he or she could be the right coach for you. Authors, speakers, and online business owners generally offer some form of a coaching program available to the public. Simply visit their website to search for offers.

Another way to find a mentor is to do something for them. Coaches are extremely busy people, so there is a lot to be done. If your favorite online entrepreneur doesn't offer a formal coaching program, then providing something of value to them is your next best option. Take a look at how Charlie Hoehn got Internet titan Tim Ferriss to be his mentor by simply adding value and contributing to his business efforts:

Case Study: Charlie Hoehn

After graduating from college during a recession, Charlie Hoehn had trouble finding a job. He was reportedly rejected by multiple companies, including a company where he had completed an internship. After months of disappointment, Charlie decided to try a different approach. Instead of sending his resume to companies (like every other college graduate), Charlie decided to offer free work to some of his biggest role models. One of these people was Tim Ferriss, author of the mega-bestseller *The 4-Hour Workweek*.

In his book *Recession-Proof Graduate*, Charlie recommends researching your target mentor and reaching out to them. This is the exact strategy that Charlie used to gain Tim as a mentor. He leveraged a relationship with Ramit Sethi, a friend of Tim's, to gain an email introduction. Here is a portion of the email that Charlie used to gain Tim Ferriss as a mentor:

——— Forwarded message ———
From: Charlie Hoehn
Date: Wed, Jul 30, 2008 at 11:25 PM
Subject: Re: Response requested
To: Ramit Sethi

Hi Ramit-

Below is the email I wrote up for Tim Ferriss. Thanks again so much for your insight on how to approach this, and for your willingness to pass it along. If you have any suggestions, I'd love to hear them. Also, I'd be willing to help you out in any of the ways I outlined below.

Mr. Ferriss-

After visiting your site countless times since May '07, I've come up with a few suggestions that could improve your readers' experience. Here are two of the things I think you need…

2) A more dynamic "About" page: Currently, this page starts off with a quote about you from Albert Pope, followed by three thumbnail pictures of your face and a great deal of text outlining your achievements. While your credentials are impressive, this page doesn't really capture your personality or the lifestyle you've designed for yourself.

What it would take: You need a video, between 2 and 5 minutes, that captures the excitement that comes with lifestyle design. The video would showcase exciting things you've done (skydiving, tango, motorcycling, etc.), and would be a great way to show your readers that you are the real deal.

How I could help: I can make this video for you for free. I've been editing video for more than four years, and started a business in creating movies for special events. All I would need to make your video are great pictures and videos of you. The more they show the human side of you, the better.

What the benefits are to you: Reading something is fine, but an image is far more powerful. This video will establish an even deeper credibility with your new (and old) readers. Even if you end up deciding that it's not right for your site, you'll still be getting a great video about you that would normally cost several hundred dollars. If you like my work, we can discuss other ways to implement videos into your site (including higher quality and more exciting videos for your blog).

What's the pay-off for me – I would learn firsthand about your methods for extreme productivity and efficiency. Reading has given me a solid level of understanding, but actually seeing it would help me comprehend it more fully. Second, you've already done what I want to become: an entrepreneur who travels a lot. Working with you would allow me to really mentally shift gears and help move me towards my goals faster.

That being said, I have a great deal of respect for you and the things you've done. I think it'd be brilliant to work with you in some way, but if it doesn't work out, no hard feelings. Thanks for your time, Tim, and I hope to talk with you again soon.

Charlie

As you can see from the email, Charlie offered Tim free video production services in exchange for a mentorship. By mentioning that he has "been editing video for more than four years," Charlie proves that he is not just some random guy out in cyberspace. By stating that "this video will establish an even deeper credibility with your new (and old) readers," Charlie explains how his expertise can specifically benefit Tim's business.

At the end of the email, Charlie perfectly describes the role of a mentor when he explains to Tim how this mentorship would benefit him as the provider of the service. Charlie so eloquently describes everything I have been trying to teach you in this chapter when he said the following: "**You've already done what I want to become**: an entrepreneur who travels a lot. Working with you would allow me to mentally shift gears and help **move me towards my goals faster.**"

In order to receive coaching, you can pay a mentor or work for them for free. Having a coach to guide you will skyrocket your success and help you create unlimited online wealth much sooner than you could by yourself.

***Sign up** to get a free consultation to evaluate your online business by going to my website: www.DotComProfitBook.com and sign into the Bonus area to get a **Free One-on-One strategy session**.

Chapter 8:

Bet on Yourself

In order to create unlimited online wealth, you must bet on yourself. Success in online business is 30% strategy and 70% belief. This means that you have to *believe* that you can succeed regardless of your present-day circumstances. Everyone is an expert at something. Believing that you have something of value to offer will skyrocket your online business earnings and put you on the path to dot com profits.

"You become what you believe."

– Oprah Winfrey

After you've mastered the art of belief, you must then understand how to make all of the strategies work. A strategy only works if you understand it, absorb it, and apply it. This means that you must first thoroughly *understand* all of the steps required to run a profitable online business. Next, you have to *absorb* the information so that you can seamlessly transfer the strategies into your own business. Finally, you must *apply* all of the principles outlined in this book. Your online business will not grow unless you take massive action.

When taking action, you must remember to think big. Working for yourself requires that you have a clear vision of the future. Bet on yourself by having big dreams.

Dream Big

One thing that all successful people have in common is that they dream big. In addition to self-belief, you must have big dreams in order to build a profitable online business. Leave small thinking to the employees who exist only to follow instructions and to work on someone else's dreams. Walmart employees work to fulfill Sam Walton's dreams. The team at Virgin Group work to fulfill Richard Branson's dreams. By owning your own business, you get to live out *your* dreams on *your* watch.

Making massive dot com profits requires that you have a clear vision of success. You must know what you want so clearly that you can see it when you close your eyes. Your dreams for the future must be so deeply rooted that they ignite a passion inside you. The idea of unlimited online wealth must dominate your thought processes by being on your mind at all times. The only way to achieve your dreams of online wealth is to turn your desires into a burning obsession. That burning obsession will make your dreams of dot com profits much more attainable.

After you initially dream big, you must dream even bigger! Multi-millionaire and online business titan Grant Cardone calls this the 10X rule. In fact, he wrote an entire book called *The 10X Rule*! Grant recommends that we take our goals and multiply them by10. This means that if your goal is to make $100,000 per year in your online business, then you should 10X it to $1,000,000 per year! Would you prefer to make 6 figures or 7 figures? Although 6 figures in profits are more attainable, 7 figures forces you to stretch even more. The challenge of multiplying your ambitions ignites your critical thinking skills and puts you on the path toward financial success. Take your current dreams and multiply them by 10 in order to create unlimited online wealth.

When dreaming big, remember to think globally. The Internet gives you the power to reach customers from all around the world. This means that you should consider getting your products translated into different languages. English is a fantastic language! However, if you rely on it exclusively, you are leaving out a large segment of your market due to conventional thinking. Languages are just one piece of the puzzle. The big idea is to think globally. Brainstorm ways to serve your international customers as well as your native people. The Internet has given us unlimited access to one another. By thinking creatively, you can turn that unlimited access into unlimited wealth.

For example, you could hire someone on Elance to translate your book from English to Spanish. You could then get that same contractor to translate your sales page, your email sequence, and even your video tutorials so that you can send your Spanish-speaking customers through your Spanish sales funnel! Of course this is only one example. The idea is to use your creative thinking to expand your business globally and to create additional revenue streams in the process. Dreaming big and thinking globally will put you well on the path toward dot com profits.

Work Smart, Not Hard

When betting on yourself, you have to remember to work smart, not hard. Working smart leads to financial freedom. Working hard leads to stress and anxiety. Working smart involves leveraging other people's time and skills. Working hard involves trying to do everything on your own and risking time with your loved ones to build an online business. Continue reading to learn more about the distinction between working hard and working smart.

An online entrepreneur who works smart follows the advice written in this book. He validates his market, sells high-end products, creates multiple streams of income, outsources work he doesn't do proficiently, buys traffic with a high return on investment, and gets coaching from the best in his field. He doesn't waste time on low-priority tasks, and he creates online wealth much faster than most people.

An online entrepreneur who works hard does the exact opposite. He chooses a niche because he *thinks* it will be profitable—without ever testing the market or doing customer research. He only has one income stream (most likely an eBook) that sells for a measly $10 on Amazon. He spends months designing his own website (even though he is terrible at it), refuses to pay for traffic, and avoids getting a mentor or outsourcing because he believes that no one can do a better job than he can. He wastes years and gets nowhere.

In order to skyrocket your online business profits, you must work smart. Follow the steps in the previous chapters so that you will reach your dreams quickly. Building a profitable online business doesn't have to be strenuous and time-consuming. Use the strategies I have given you to leverage other people's knowledge and skills so that you can spend more time doing what you enjoy. Build your online wealth the smart way, not the hard way.

Take Back Control of Your Life

Betting on yourself allows you to take back control of your life. By following the principles in this book, you ensure that your time is spent doing things that really matter to you. The days of reporting to your boss are long gone. The long commutes to work, the conniving co-workers, and the overall deprivation of true happiness that you may have become accustomed to all come to an end when you decide to bet on yourself.

Building a profitable online business allows you the freedom to do whatever you desire. You can make money from your laptop (and even from your iPhone) with the press of a button. One email to your list of customers can result in thousands of dollars in revenue after only a few hours. You no longer have to worry about whether or not your boss is going to give you a raise or when you can request vacation time. The only thing you have to focus on is adding massive value to a target market on the Internet. You can earn money from anywhere and take a vacation whenever you want! In fact, several online entrepreneurs do business from paradise locations all year round!

By betting on yourself, you have chosen to create profits rather than to collect wages. You have chosen to own your own business rather than being paid to run someone else's company. Betting on yourself allows you to build assets that can be sold over and over again for years in the future. This means that you no longer have to trade time for money. Betting on yourself allows you to exchange *value* for money. You don't have a boss; instead, you will have a database of customers who know, like, and trust you. Take back your life by betting on your potential to build a profitable online business.

Make a Plan

In order to bet on yourself, you must have a solid action plan. Working online requires that you create systems that support your success. This includes having daily action steps that get you closer to your goals. You cannot succeed in this line of work without an effective system for getting things done. Your plan is what makes your big dreams come alive.

Making a plan ensures that you remain focused. It can be easy to get side-tracked when running an Internet-based company. You don't have to clock in. You have no schedule (unless you create one yourself). You are in full control of your time, and that can create more problems than one would expect. Making a plan that you follow every single day ensures that you don't lose perspective when coping with your newly-found freedom. Sticking to a plan over a long period of time is what separates the winners from the losers. You must dedicate yourself to daily action in order to achieve your long-term goal of dot com profits.

Be Patient

If you are reading this book, then you are most likely interested in creating online wealth quickly; however, you must remember to be patient. It takes time to master all of the strategies outlined here. No one creates unlimited online wealth overnight. Once you've gained the skills required to create wealth, you'll then be able to generate large profits from an idea immediately. In the meantime, however, it is wise to focus mainly on progress.

Celebrate the small wins. Hiring your first freelancer, adding a second revenue stream, and finding a mentor are all crucial steps that you should be proud of. Every action reinforces the fact that you have what it takes to build a profitable online business. Positive results allow you to gain momentum, and gaining momentum catapults your online revenue into the stratosphere!

While on this journey of unlimited online wealth, you will be tempted to compare yourself to others. You will hear success stories of many people making 6 figures *per month* while you are still striving to make 6 figures per year. But don't let this get you down. Everyone has to start somewhere. The success stories that you will hear (some even in this book) were years in the making. A lot of the success stories that you will hear highlight people who started off as epic failures.

Some of the most successful online business owners started with nothing—no money, no credibility, and no high-profile network.

The only thing you need in order to succeed is a strong desire for online wealth. If you want it badly enough, then you will succeed no matter how you begin. Just take it one step at a time. You can do this! Ramit Sethi (the guy selling a $1,000 course) started off selling a $4 eBook. After nearly a decade running an online business, his elite offers now run up to $12,000 for personal coaching! With time, you can get there, too. It's simply a matter of staying in the game.

Bet on yourself. Take back control of your life by dreaming big, making a plan, working smart, and being patient. These steps allow you to gain a sense of freedom that you may never have thought possible. Betting on yourself allows you to claim your power and live the life of your dreams. Bet on yourself and begin to create unlimited online wealth today!

Conclusion:

Take Action

In order to create unlimited online wealth, you must take massive action. Reading this book won't help you unless you apply the principles it presents. You have all of the strategies that you need. The very last step is to simply get started on your journey toward dot com profits.

Whether you are just starting out or have been doing business on the Internet for years, I'm sure you've found this information valuable. These eight chapters have provided you a crash course in online wealth generation. From finding a buying market to selling high-priced offers, I've shared with you some of my best wealth-building secrets. In order to move toward the path of dot com profits, all you have to do is take action on the steps that I've outlined for you.

With the aim of helping you generate revenue, I have written a quick summary for you. The following is an overview of the 8 steps to creating unlimited online wealth. Follow these steps and begin your journey toward dot com profits!

Step 1: Find a Buying Market

The first step to creating unlimited online wealth is to find a buying market. In order to find a buying market, you must validate your idea, understand your target market, and create your customer avatar. These actions will allow you to avoid wasting valuable time and money creating a product that no one wants. Finding a buying market virtually guarantees your online business success.

In order to validate your market, you can get product pre-sales, run pay-per-click ads, do keyword research, and search for similar products in the Amazon marketplace. Performing this critical research ahead of time will provide proof of concept and put you head and shoulders above other online business owners who simply "guess" what their market wants. Take the risk out of entrepreneurship by first validating your market.

Once you've validated your market, you must then seek to *understand* your market. There is no better way to understand your market than to identify their demographics and their psychographics. Demographics include your target customers' age, income, gender, and location. Psychographics include your target customers' hopes, fears, challenges, and aspirations. A great way to find out your customers' demographics and psychographics is to survey them and listen to their feedback.

By combining all of these strategies, you will have a clear picture of your ideal customer. In marketing, we call this archetype your customer avatar. Understanding your customer avatar will allow you to appropriately name your products and services while avoiding the urge to advertise to the wrong people. Understanding your ideal customers can save you years of pain and suffering.

Step 2: Position Your Brand at Top Market

The second step to creating unlimited online wealth is to position your brand at top market. You can do this by sharing your story, developing your USP, and becoming an expert. The right positioning makes your customers say, "Wow!" It allows you to brand your name or your business and to differentiate yourself from your competition. Positioning your brand at top market allows you to attract high-quality customers.

When sharing your story, you should focus on defining moments. Highlight your challenges, your obstacles, your wins, and your losses. This allows you to build a deep connection with your audience and makes you more relatable. Sharing your story makes customers trust you. This trust arises because they see you as an old friend who is *just like them*. Share your story in order to build your brand.

In the world of online business, there are a lot of copycats. People have gotten used to the idea of everyone being the same. In order to distinguish yourself, you must develop your unique selling proposition (USP). An effective USP immediately explains how you are different or better than your competitors. It is a phrase or a tagline that accurately describes your brand and establishes you as an authority. Having a USP proves that you are not like everyone else in your market. Develop your USP and get treated like a VIP!

Possibly the best way to position your brand at top market is to become an expert. Being an expert allows you to demand respect and be perceived as a credible source of information. Showcase your expertise by writing a book and being everywhere. Few people have more credibility than an author. Write down your best thoughts and then share your expertise on multiple platforms. Becoming an expert will immediately position your brand at top market.

Step 3: Sell High-Priced Offers

The third step to creating unlimited online wealth is to sell high-priced offers. You can sell high-priced offers by focusing on product modalities, high profit margins, and perceived value. These factors all determine how soon you will be able to generate dot com profits. High-priced products and services attract high-quality people who value your time, your knowledge, and your skills. Sell high-priced offers and begin to generate wealth.

Your offer's modality greatly determines its price point. The four main modalities are text, audio, video, and live events. Text-based products such as books and newsletters are sold at the lowest price point. Audio programs typically retail for a higher price than text-based products. Video courses are the most expensive digital products. In-person events and one-on-one coaching have the highest perceived value; therefore, live events can be sold at much higher prices. Your ability to sell high-priced offers is totally dependent upon your offer's modality and perceived value.

In order to skyrocket your online business earnings, you should focus on high profit margins. It takes the same effort to get 10 high-quality customers as it does to get 10,000 lower quality customers. Regardless of its price point, each product has the same sales process. Focus on high profit margins in order to avoid burnout and to generate online wealth much faster.

As I mentioned in the section on product modality, your ability to sell high-priced products is solely based on its perceived value. People will eagerly purchase your high-end products as long as you effectively communicate their value. Explain the serious amount of time and money that went into creating your product. Make your prospects understand how your knowledge, your experience, and/or your network can prevent their pain and increase their pleasure. Selling high-priced offers is the way to Internet riches!

Step 4: Create Multiple Streams of Income

The fourth step to creating unlimited online wealth is to create multiple streams of income. Having multiple revenue streams allows you to break the link between your time and your money. There are only 24 hours in a day, and having more than one revenue source maximizes your freedom. You can create multiple streams of income by utilizing affiliates and creating an integrated product suite.

An integrated product suite is simply a collection of related products, each of which solves a different problem or satisfies a different need for your target market. These products and services should vary in both price and modality. Product suites often begin with free content that leads to higher-priced offers.

After you've built your suite, you should then get other people to promote your products. Affiliate partnerships multiply your impact and quadruple your income. Give your partners an attractive commission, and watch the sales come pouring in! Creating a series of related products and integrating affiliate promotions around them is the path to online wealth.

Step 5: Automate and Streamline Your Business

The fifth step to creating unlimited online wealth is to automate and streamline your business. Automation allows you to generate income 24 hours per day, seven days per week. When streamlining your business, be sure to steer clear of Superhero Syndrome—the disease of trying to do everything yourself. Avoid this by outsourcing any work that is not the best use of your own time. Create sales funnels so that you can systematize your business and put more focus on creating additional revenue streams.

One of the best ways to streamline your business is to build a solid team. During your journey to dot com profits, you will need people to handle your email, design your website, and complete other activities that you are not equipped to do by yourself. That is why you should hire professionals on websites like Fiverr, Elance, and Virtual Staff Finder. Build a solid team and generate wealth sooner.

Systematize your business by creating "street-level" documents and sales funnels. "Street-level" documents illustrate the step-by-step procedure for every critical function in your business. They allow you to easily train new employees if something happens to a member of your team.

In addition to creating the all of the above products, you should also build marketing sales funnels. Creating unlimited online wealth requires that you have customers going through your funnel at all times. Sell all of the products in your suite by using customer relationship management (CRM) software to scale your business. Applying these strategies will take your profits to the next level.

Step 6: Generate Traffic

The sixth step to creating unlimited online wealth is to generate traffic. None of the strategies I've outlined for you will work unless you have qualified traffic going to your offers. You can find qualified prospects by advertising on search engines and social media outlets. When paying for traffic, be sure to know your ROI and collect contact information.

You can purchase advertising space on search engines like Google, Yahoo!, and Bing. You can also buy customers using social media sites like Facebook, Twitter, and LinkedIn. Paying for traffic allows you to immediately validate your market and create instant revenue.

When purchasing traffic, it is essential that you know your return on investment (ROI). Knowing your ROI helps you avoid losing money and wasting time. It is OK to spend $1 in order to make $3. You should continue to spend money as long as you are making money. Simply track your profits and losses to determine whether or not to continue with your advertising campaign.

In addition to paying for traffic and tracking your ROI, you should also be collecting contact information. Having a database of paying customers allows you to generate sales over and over again. With a simple email to your list, you could generate thousands of dollars in sales in just a few hours. Capture email addresses in order to have repeat buyers who skyrocket your online business earnings.

Step 7: Get Coaching

The seventh step to creating unlimited online wealth is to get coaching. Finding a mentor who has already done what you want to achieve will fast-track your online success. Coaches help keep you accountable. They provide a blueprint that you can follow in order to achieve similar results. Mentors help you achieve your goals much faster than you can by yourself.

Be sure to seek coaching from a mentor, not an advisor. An advisor typically has valuable information, but they usually lack personal experience. A mentor typically has years of "in-the-trenches" experience doing what you want to do. You can build a relationship with a mentor by either paying them or by doing free work in exchange for guidance.

Mentors give you the blueprint to success and provide accountability on your journey to dot com profits. They keep you on track and help you avoid procrastination. Mentors help you avoid some of the inevitable pitfalls that come with building a business. Get coaching to fast-track your success.

Step 8: Bet on Yourself

The last step to creating unlimited online wealth is to bet on yourself. This means that you should dream big, work smart, and follow a proven plan of action. You must decide that you will no longer trade time for money— because you value your freedom more than a steady paycheck. Online business allows you to create multiple revenue streams, but only if you have the courage to take action.

All successful people dream big. They believe in themselves and in their ability to create the life they were born to live. In order to build a profitable online business, you must have a clear vision of your success. After you have a clear vision, you must 10x that vision in order to get where you ultimately want to be.

When betting on yourself, remember to work smart, not hard. Outsource monotonous tasks, sell high-priced products, and always validate your market. Don't spend time on a task unless it directly affects your bottom line. Follow the advice in this book so that you can leverage other people's time and expertise in order to build your online empire.

Finally, make a plan and stick to it. True success is a result of positive habits. Be sure to move at least one step closer to your goals every single day. This allows you to gain momentum and skyrocket your earning potential. Find a buying market. Position your brand at top market. Sell high-priced offers. Create multiple streams of income. Automate your business. Generate traffic. Get coaching. And bet on yourself. Following these steps will allow you to fulfill your dreams of creating unlimited online wealth.

Begin your journey to dot com profits today!

Bibliography

"Building a $4,260 Per Month Kindle Publishing Business." The Side Hustle Show.

Burchard, Brendon. *The Millionaire Messenger: Make a Difference and a Fortune Sharing Your Advice.* New York: Free Press, 2011.

Cardone, Grant. *The 10X Rule: The Only Difference between Success and Failure.* Hoboken: Wiley, 2011.

DiPiazza, Daniel. "Hacking Elance: The Step-by-Step Guide to How I Made $23,700 in 4 Weeks." Under30CEO. 6 June 2013.

DiPiazza, Daniel. "What's Your Biggest Challenge?" Rich 20 Something.

Ducker, Chris. *Virtual Freedom: How to Work with Virtual Staff to Buy More Time, Become More Productive, and Build Your Dream Business.* Dallas: BenBella Books, 2014.

Dumas, John Lee. "How I Built a $98,993 Sales Funnel Using LeadPages." LeadPages.

"EOFire's September 2014 Monthly Income Report." Entrepreneur on Fire.

Hoehn, Charlie. "12 Lessons Learned While Marketing *The 4-Hour Body.*" The 4-Hour Workweek.

Hoehn, Charlie. *Recession Proof Graduate: How to Get the Job You Want By Doing Free Work.* CharlieHoehn.com, 2014.

"Oprah gives away 276 new Pontiacs." CNN Money. 13 September 2004.

Paige, Tim. "How Valerie Shoopman Combined Two Tactics to Generate $61,000 in Just Four Days." LeadPages.

"Selena Soo on over-delivering for amazing results." Entrepreneur on Fire.

Shih, Jenny. "Curious about B-School? Here's my 100% honest review." Jenny Shih.

Soo, Selena. "5 Ways to Gain Instant Credibility in Your Industry." DailyWorth. 23 December 2013.

Tardy, Jamie. *The Eventual Millionaire: How Anyone Can Be an Entrepreneur and Successfully Grow Their Startup*. Hoboken: Wiley, 2014.

Vaynerchuk, Gary. "Want to get advertisers on your blog?" YouTube. 2 April 2012.

Wagner, Eric. "Five Reasons 8 Out of 10 Businesses Fail." Forbes. 12 September 2013.

About the Author

Ivan Ho has been featured on the cover of *Internet Marketing Magazine* and has coached and mentored hundreds of people around the world, showing them the right strategies and blueprint to succeed online.

Ivan is also the author of *Dot Com Experts* and *25 Expert Tips to Blogging Success*. He has also created two online teaching platforms called Blogging Business Tips, an online tutorial blog, and also OMT Wired Up, an online podcast featured on iTunes that teaches successful tips and strategies on how to make money online.

Ivan's online tutorials include:

A One-on-One 8-Week Coaching Session
How to Create High-Converting Sales Funnels
The Profit Blogging Blueprint Tutorial Program
Facebook Ads Domination
Affiliate Marketing for Beginners

Stay in touch with Ivan:

Email: ivan@imvbusiness.com
Blog: www.BloggingBusinessTips.com
Podcast: www.bloggingbusinesstips.com/go/itunes
Facebook: www.facebook.com/bloggingbusinesstips
Twitter: www.twitter.com/blogbiztips
LinkedIn: www.bloggingbusinesstips.com/go/linkedin
Google Plus: www.plus.google.com/+Bloggingbusinesstips

www.DotComProfitBook.com

www.ingramcontent.com/pod-product-compliance
Ingram Content Group UK Ltd.
Pitfield, Milton Keynes, MK11 3LW, UK
UKHW020134250726
13967UKWH00002B/658

9 781772 770063